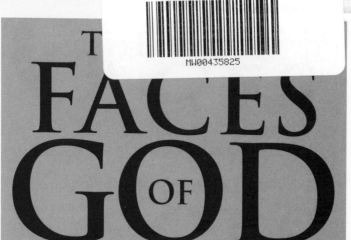

# THE FACES OF GOD

## PICTURES OF THE INTIMACY
## GOD DESIRES WITH HIS CHILDREN

Other books by this author:

*Practical Pointers to Personal Prayer*
*Sanctuary Secrets to Personal Prayer*
*Sensing His Presence, Hearing His Voice*
*What to Say* (with Daniel O'Ffill)
*When We Pray for Others*
*The Worshiping Heart:*
   *Key to a Personal Relationship With God*

To order, call 1-800-765-6955.

Visit us at www.reviewandherald.com for information on other Review and Herald® products.

# THE MANY
# FACES
# GOD OF

## PICTURES OF THE INTIMACY
## GOD DESIRES WITH HIS CHILDREN

CARROL JOHNSON SHEWMAKE

REVIEW AND HERALD® PUBLISHING ASSOCIATION
HAGERSTOWN, MD 21740

The author assumes full responsibility for the accuracy of all facts and quotations as cited in this book.

Unless otherwise noted, Scripture quotations are from the *Holy Bible, New International Version.* Copyright © 1973, 1978, 1984, International Bible Society. Used by permission of Zondervan Bible Publishers.

Texts credited to Clear Word are from *The Clear Word,* copyright © 2000 by Jack J. Blanco.

Texts credited to NKJV are from the New King James Version. Copyright © 1979, 1980, 1982 by Thomas Nelson, Inc. Used by permission. All rights reserved.

Verses marked TLB are taken from *The Living Bible,* copyright © 1971 by Tyndale House Publishers, Wheaton, Ill. Used by permission.

This book was
Edited by Gerald Wheeler
Copyedited by Jan Schleifer and James Cavil
Designed by The Idea Works
Photos by Joel D. Springer, PhotoDisc, and Stockbyte
Typeset: 11/14 Garamond Book

PRINTED IN U.S.A.

08 07 06 05 04          5 4 3 2 1

**R&H Cataloging Service**
Shewmake, Carrol Johnson, 1927-
        The many faces of God: pictures of the intimacy God desires with His children.

        1. God.   I. Title.

231

ISBN 0-8280-1785-9

# Contents

## *How Can I Visualize God?*

Few people attempt to draw a picture of God the Father. His Son, Jesus, who walked here on earth, yes, many artists depict Him. But God the Father? God is a Spirit who lives in a high and holy place. In the New Testament when Philip asked Jesus to show him the Father, Jesus told the disciples that if they had seen Him, they had observed the Father, too. Jesus also told them that the Holy Spirit was to take His place on earth when He returned to heaven. Evidently, to know one member of the Godhead is to know Them all.

As a child growing up in a Christian home that included morning and evening worship and weekly church attendance, I had a picture of God that was simple. I felt secure in His love, confident of His power and authority.

But when I began to study the Bible as an adult, I discovered I had seemingly unanswerable questions. As a young pastor's wife I remember telling someone that as far as I was concerned, the compilers of the Bible could have just left out Exodus through 2 Chronicles. All that shedding of animal blood; those horrible wars! I couldn't handle the violence of the Bible. It seemed to me that the majority of Scripture focused on war, while I longed for peace. Was God a deity of peace or of war?

In reading the Bible, I skimmed past the books of the

ancient prophets—even Revelation in the New Testament. Who could understand the significance of all those strange creatures? Schoolwork had come easily for me in childhood, and I seldom dealt with weighty subjects. I liked things to be quick and easy. Thus I left Daniel and Revelation and the majority of prophetic books for my minister husband to understand and to explain.

As a school librarian I valued order. Although I didn't know the answers to all the questions the students asked me, I knew how to find them. The whole library system existed to make it easy to locate answers. Why wasn't the Bible like that? Some books of the Bible seemed to have no relationship whatsoever with the others around them. Surely whoever edited the Bible could have arranged the books in better order! Even within a book, just when I seemed to find something that helped me in understanding a concept, the writer would change the subject. I had a hard time following through on themes—let alone discovering answers to my questions about God. What was it that held the 66 diverse books of the Bible together and made them a complete holy book? Somewhere I was missing a vital clue.

Our ministerial life was busy. I loved working for the Lord—but I knew I needed to find answers to some of my questions. As a result I spent wakeful nights in prayer. "Lord, show me truth or I will teach error," I petitioned. When I had to wait in the car for my husband, I prayed. And when I waited for a doctor's appointment, I prayed. I wrote lists of God's character traits on scraps of paper. Constantly I searched Scripture.

It was then—in the midst of my busy life—that I discovered the missing clue to making 66 books written by numerous writers into one Holy Bible. For a class in continuing education I read the complete Bible, book by book, with one specific question to ask of each book: What is the picture of God I find in this book of the Bible? Then I was to write a brief report answering that question.

As I explored the inspired books with this question in mind, I realized for the first time that an underlying continuity did run throughout the entire 66 books. In the very first book of the Old Testament I found a golden thread of intimacy between God and the human race that continued through all the rest, glowing even more brightly when it reached Revelation.

"I will be your God," the Almighty promised, "and you will be My people." This coupling of God and humanity was as impossible to break as it would be for the sun to disappear and never rise again. Again and again throughout Scripture God reiterated this same yearning desire for a love relationship with humanity. At the beginning He emphasized its importance by wording it in "covenant" language—a legal document that cannot be broken. Later He incorporated His intense desire for intimacy with us into word pictures of various human relationships and the life of nature around us.

I have never been the same since that discovery. It's almost as though I see God with new eyes as I read the Bible. His longing for intimacy and understanding reaches out to me in every passage. It invades my meditation, my prayers, and my writing. True, my questions about God have not all received answers—but then I don't understand everything about my husband, either, and he is a human being like me. Thus I can expect that learning to know God will continue throughout my earthly lifetime—and doubtless through eternity. But my mental block in reading Scripture has vanished. Now I can explore the entire Bible with an open mind, realizing that God's purpose is to reveal, not to conceal. God teaches me some of His most precious lessons from those books I once thought should have been left out!

As I begin writing this book I am excited about pulling together the many faces that God shows of Himself throughout Scripture. What I want to portray is the reality of knowing Him as a dear and intimate friend, closer even than any family member.

As I continue to read and study the Bible I realize that it isn't always easy to understand what God is like—especially for a beginner. Human words can never perfectly explain divine things. Three principles have helped me to face this dilemma.

First, the illumination of the Holy Spirit must always accompany the reading of the Bible. Only the Holy Spirit can put into our minds a perfect picture of God.

Second, we need to realize that God, understanding human nature so well, purposefully makes us search the Bible to discover His character. He knows that our comprehension will grow only as we exert our minds in the exploration.

Third, no one verse of the Bible ever stands alone. I look for other passages to clarify or expand what I think the verse in question is saying. And if I can find none, I may be misinterpreting the verse.

In one place God gives us one word picture that shows us one facet of Himself, then another portrait in some other place. It is only by putting all our small snapshots together that we begin to glimpse His fullness and majesty.

This book is the product of my personal search for the golden thread of God's desire for intimacy with humanity. It is my hope that you, the reader, will begin to taste the goodness of God for yourself, to feel His great love reaching out, and to respond with your own yearning for Him! May this book be the beginning of your individual exploration for the many faces of God.

## The Longing God:
## Father, Son, and Holy Spirit

Let's imagine God the Father, God the Son, and God the Holy Spirit early in earth's history, long before the writing of the Bible, discussing how to reveal Themselves to sinful humanity.

"It's hard for humans to visualize God," the Son commented.

"It's true," the Spirit added. "They have difficulty imagining something they can't see with their physical eyes."

"We've taken care of that, remember?" the Father asked, looking lovingly at His Son. "Even before Adam and Eve rebelled against us, You offered, should it be needed, to become one of them and pay the price for their rebellion. That way You can reveal Us to them."

"Yes, but think how many generations of humans are going to live and die before the time is right for that," the Son observed sadly. "How are they going to know how very much We love and care for them?"

"If only they could all grasp the intimacy with Us that is already possible for them now by faith," the Spirit sighed.

"We need to put it into words that they can easily comprehend," the Father suggested.

"Word pictures!" the Son almost shouted. "That's the

11

idea. We'll choose humans who are faithful to Us—"

"And inspire them to put our thoughts accurately and poetically into human words," the Spirit finished for Him. "That's My job," the Spirit continued happily, "and I love it! I love wooing humans with divine love. I love it especially when they open up their hearts and let Me enter in and fill them with Our presence. Then it's not hard to help them understand how much We love them and want to have an intimate relationship with them."

"Yes, it's the others who are the problem," the Father said. "Those who turn their faces from Us and hold their hearts closed against Us."

"Let's find as many ways as they can possibly understand to describe intimate relationships, and put them into human words," the Son urged.

"We'll do even better than that," the Father replied. "We'll make every word picture a copy of an actual earthly relationship."

The Spirit was excited. "Of course, of course," He said, "that will make My job so much easier. I can just remind them of what they call 'real life'—and tell them that God is even more than that!"

"Let's give them a comprehensive picture early on," the Son suggested. "Something that will outline the whole of human history and offer them hope and expectancy."

"We can choose the descendants of one man and woman who worship the Creator-God to become a special chosen people to reveal Us to the rest of the world," the Father added.

The Son smiled. "I like that. Do You suppose We could give them a living illustration of Our ministry for them?"

"Perhaps We could have them make a model of the heavenly sanctuary that they could actually become involved with," the Father proposed.

"Wonderful idea!" the Spirit agreed. "We can let Our glory rest upon it like a cloud."

The Father, deep in contemplation, turned to the Son. "And through that illustration We can describe the scope of Your ministry so they'll be receptive to You when You come to earth as a human being to save them from their sins. That should be encouraging and make them turn to Us more readily."

"Not only My ministry and life, Father," added the Son, "but We could let the model of the sanctuary illustrate their individual lives and the personal plan We have for their salvation. They'll be able to visualize how We can live within them through the Holy Spirit."

"Oh, this is a very good plan!" all Three responded with one voice and heart.

Of course, it didn't happen just like that. Yet the divine plan to reveal God to humanity is visible throughout inspired Scripture. And for anyone who has ears to hear and eyes to see spiritual things, God's great longing and love for a close relationship with each human is an open invitation to enter into intimacy with our Creator.

## PART I

## *"I Am Your God and You Are My People"*

All-powerful God, Ruler of the universe,
eternal, immortal, invisible—three in one—
Can it be that You are truly seeking sinful humanity?
Is it possible that You long for us?
Call for us? Died for us?
Have You chosen us to be Your very own?
Can we truly be Your people?
Is that possible?
Do You delight in us,
Sing over us?
Can we even now—here on sinful earth—
walk with You daily,
hear Your voice,
talk with You heart-to-heart?
Have You a future plan for us
to rejoice
in Your companionship
forever?
Are You truly our God?

## CHAPTER 1

## *He Chose Us for His Very Own!*

He did! Yes, He did! He chose us for His very own. Not only did God create our world and everything in it—designing humanity in the very image of Himself—but He also bought us back from the slavery of sin, the price being the death of His only Son, Jesus. That's the value Heaven placed upon the human race. We were chosen from the very beginning.

When I discovered the central theme of the Bible—that the Creator of the world selected sinful humanity to be His very own—it overwhelmed me. It was easy for me to picture God delighting in the perfect Adam and Eve that He had Himself created in His own image—but it was incomprehensible to me that He could still love and cherish their sinful and rebellious offspring. Reading the Bible through, looking for—and finding again and again—the assurance that God's love for His creation has never changed, despite their rebellion and sin, has made a vast difference in my spiritual life.

Although the picture of God that we find woven throughout the 66 books of the Bible is definitely that of a high and holy Creator God—one true God—yet we continually find Him stooping low to reach the weakest sinner. The prophet Isaiah says of Him:

"For this is what the high and lofty One says—
he who lives forever, whose name is holy:
'I live in a high and holy place,
but also with him who is contrite and lowly in spirit,
to revive the spirit of the lowly
and to revive the heart of the contrite.'"

—Isaiah 57:15

The incredible—and almost unbelievable—message of the Bible is that this great awesome God has a love for and a desire to communicate with the people He created. Not only does Scripture stress His Creatorship and power, but it tells us that He longs to have an intimate relationship with us. He redeemed us for a purpose: to relate with Him throughout eternity. The theme runs throughout Scripture like a golden ribbon: "I am your God and you are My people."

Because of Adam and Eve's sin-damaged hearts, and all humanity's thereafter, we can no longer stand in the visible presence of divinity and live. But God's grace devised a way for the repentant human race to commune with Him. With the presence of the Holy Spirit in their renewed hearts they are able to reach the courts of heaven through prayer— heart-to-heart in place of face-to-face. *God never leaves His people alone—He is always by their side.*

The Bible records that in spite of God's grace so freely given, evil continued to flourish throughout the earth as generation after generation tried to fill their spiritual emptiness with selfish pleasures. Yet in every generation the Lord always had a few who were loyal to Him and represented Him to the world.

When the time came that almost every human thought was evil, God stepped into human history and destroyed the earth by a flood, saving only loyal Noah, his wife, three sons, and their wives to repopulate the earth with people who would once again serve the true God (Gen. 6:5, 13, 18).

When the rainwaters stopped and the earth dried off, God promised Noah that He would never again destroy the earth by a flood. To make it easier for Noah and his family to remember His promise, God gave them a visible sign: amid the colorless landscape of the empty earth God flung a glorious iridescent rainbow across the sky (Gen. 9:12-16). The rainbow would forever guarantee God's faithfulness to His people.

But even the Flood did not stop the increase of evil. God never uses force, but leaves human beings free to choose whom they will serve. Many of Noah's descendants became as wicked as those God had destroyed. Yet He always had a remnant who served Him.

God took Abraham of the line of Shem, son of Noah, with his wife, Sarah, away from the wicked city of their ancestors to dwell as pilgrims in a country that God promised would one day belong to their descendants. To Abraham, God revealed His plan to establish from his descendants a people through whom He could spread the knowledge of the true God throughout the earth.

" 'I will establish my covenant as an everlasting covenant between me and you and your descendants after you for the generations to come, to be your God and the God of your descendants after you' " (Gen. 17:7), He told Abraham.

Today we would call this a pact or treaty. The Lord made an agreement, signed by two parties, Abraham and God, and notarized by the universe. God is still honoring this covenant. He renewed it to Isaac, Abraham's son, and then again to Jacob, his grandson—all worshipers of the true God. His purpose was to have a people through whom He could display His power, His splendor, and His love.

Woven throughout the entire Bible, a golden ribbon of grace brings hope to every generation. God's loving voice continually calls, "I am your God and you are My people."

The numerous gods of the majority of the inhabitants of the world were often perceived to be indifferent or even cruel. Although the people worshiped them, it was not from love, but from fear. Through Abraham's relationship with the great God who loved and protected those who worshiped Him, his descendants and the people around them caught a glimpse of the omnipotent God, a being of compassion and love, a deity who intervened in behalf of His people.

We cannot understand the big picture that God clearly sees as He views not only the present, but the past and the future. As humans we observe it in stages: Since we live in the "present," we look backward to discover the picture of God that the Old Testament portrays. In the New Testament we receive our clearest picture of God in the life of Jesus and find that He is not only "past" but a part of the "present." Then, studying prophecies in both the Old and New Testaments, we try to visualize the "future." Yet here in our "present" we catch only dimly a glimpse of the whole picture that God sees as He contemplates past, present, and future all at once.

A friend showed me a picture that illustrates the difference between our understanding and God's. It was a simple drawing of a town, a railroad depot, and a train filled with passengers leaving the station. The train track followed along the side of a hill, curving around its edge and disappearing from sight. The passengers in the moving train could no longer view the town (the past), nor could they see around the hill (the future). Their limited awareness consisted of the terrain around the track and their side of the hill (the present). But above the town, train, and hill an airplane flew over the scene, the pilot scanning for a moment the past, present, and future of the passengers in one swift comprehensive sweep.[1]

No wonder God can work to turn evil into good!

When one of Abraham's descendants, Joseph, was sold by his jealous brothers into slavery in Egypt, God protected and guided his life. Through Joseph the Lord brought Jacob and his children and their families into Egypt as witnesses of the true God to that pagan nation. In heaven we may one day talk with men and women from Egypt who learned to know Abraham's God from their association with his descendants. Joseph told his brothers as he forgave them, "You meant it for harm, but God meant it for good" (see Gen. 45:1-8).

Yet later that same nation forced Abraham's descendants into slavery, and God allowed them to remain in bondage for hundreds of years. Why would a loving God allow the people He had especially chosen to be His own to be held in servitude by a pagan nation? Let's look for the big picture of God in this story.

Sometimes we find the answer to our questions only by looking *beyond* the specific Bible narrative to God's basic character. As I did so I began to see the immensity of a God who sees the end from the beginning—a deity who knows what will result in the best good for all humanity.

God believes in individual choice. He reads the heart, knows the future, and brings good out of evil.

He has never given up on His original plan to have a universe filled with created beings with whom He can converse throughout eternity. His plan is to have a people who—although retaining their free will—have *chosen* to be the people of God forever.

21

At every turn of history human beings have hindered God's plan. An agreement must always have at least two sides. Even when His people were slaves in Egypt, the Lord kept His side of the original compact. "I am your God," He said, "forever and ever. I will never leave you." God has always been faithful. Through the ages He has longed to hear the people He has chosen to be His very own respond, "You are my God." But instead they have forgotten Him and have followed after the gods of the nations around them.

But nothing ever takes God by surprise. He had told Abraham years before that his descendants would be slaves for 400 years in a foreign country before they would become a great nation. God's purpose for His chosen people has always been forwarded by whatever circumstances surround them.

While the Hebrew people were still slaves in Egypt He renewed His covenant promise to Moses, another descendant of Abraham. Listen to the glorious promise the Lord made to the slaves through Moses: "I will take you as *my own people, and I will be your God.* Then you will know that I am the Lord your God, who brought you out from under the yoke of the Egyptians. And I will bring you to the land I swore with uplifted hand to give to Abraham, to Isaac and to Jacob. I will give it to you as a possession. I am the Lord" (Ex. 6:7, 8).

Seemingly insurmountable obstacles mean nothing to God. In fact, they only add to His glory when He delivers His people.

In his youth Moses became acquainted with the numerous gods of the Egyptians. Because of his place in the court of Egypt he recognized the thralldom the gods demanded and the depravity of idol worship. He also knew the frightening power ascribed to the Egyptian deities.

But the Bible also relates the miraculous circumstances that made it possible for Moses, adopted son of Pharaoh's daughter, to have his birth mother, who served the true God—the Creator of the earth, all-powerful, all-wise—raise him in her faith (Ex. 2). Thus he heard the stories, passed down through the generations, of how God had called Abraham out from among idol worshipers and promised to make his offspring a great nation. Moses was familiar with the account of how God gave the childless Abraham and Sarah in their old age a miracle son to fulfill His divine promise (Gen. 21). Because he himself was a descendant of Abraham and Sarah, Moses knew the story was true. His relatives had become a huge nation, but a nation long held in slavery to the Egyptians. In fact, as a young man he had felt sure that the Hebrew God was preparing him to deliver his people from slavery. But that had not happened, and he had been forced to flee Egypt for his life and make a whole new existence for himself among desert dwellers. And now he was old.

When Moses realized that God was serious about sending him in his old age to deliver the slaves, he was appalled! He felt totally incapable of being a leader. But the divine plan was that God would be the leader and Moses only the intermediary. We learn much from the story of Moses. When God summons us to do something, He enables us to finish the job. He had called Moses in his youth. Now God enabled him in his old age to complete the mission originally given him to do.

God is always faithful, and constantly encouraged the people through Moses. "For you are a people holy to the Lord your God. The Lord your God has chosen you out of all the peoples on the face of the earth to be his people, his treasured possession" (Deut. 7:6).

In Leviticus we find Moses saying much the same, this time emphasizing Israel's responsibilities: "You are to be holy to me because I, the Lord, am holy, and I have set you apart from the nations to be my own" (Lev. 20:26).

God, the omnipotent being who dwells in high and holy places, chose not one person but a large and motley crowd of people to be His very own, to reveal Him to the world. He gave them a country at the crossroads of the then-known world so that everyone could have the opportunity to hear about the God of the Israelites. Through His people God's glory was to fill the whole earth.

He had chosen them to be His own!

That was in Old Testament times. But what about us?

I was delighted to find in the New Testament two companion verses to the Old Testament promise:

"For the grace of God that brings salvation has appeared to all men. It teaches us to say 'No' to ungodliness and worldly passions, and to live self-controlled, upright and godly lives in this present age, while we wait for the blessed hope—the glorious appearing of our great God and Savior, Jesus Christ, who gave himself for us to redeem us from all wickedness and to purify for himself a people that are his very own, eager to do what is good" (Titus 2:11-14).

"Long ago, even before he made the world, God chose us to be his very own, through what Christ would do for us; he decided then to make us holy in his eyes, without a single fault—we who stand before him covered with his love. His unchanging plan has always been to adopt us into his own family by sending Jesus Christ to die for us. And he did this because he wanted to!" (Eph. 1:4, 5, TLB).

In the New Testament we find that God still has a people.

True, many Jews failed to keep fully their side of the covenant He made with them. But God's plans went steadily forward. When the New Testament religious leaders rejected the Son of God, sorrowfully He had to let them go. Remember, God uses love, not force. The apostle Paul wrote about God's faithfulness:

> "Here is a trustworthy saying:
> If we died with him,
>> we will also live with him;
> if we endure,
>> we will also reign with him.
> If we disown him,
>> He will also disown us;
> if we are faithless,
>> he will remain faithful,
>> for he cannot disown himself."
> —2 Timothy 2:11-13

The faithlessness of some of physical Israel led God to choose spiritual Israel—a group of people from every nation, tribe, and language who of their own free will choose Him as their Savior. But the Lord has never changed: His covenant is still the same, though the recipient of His favor has been altered.

I never tire of reading about God's love for His people. Whenever I find a reference to the intimate love relationship He so obviously desires to have with human beings, I feel I have found a love letter addressed to me. Yes, God loves *me!* Yes, He is *my* God! The Creator of the universe is *my God!*

God's choice of a people—a nation of slaves—to represent Him in the ancient world still amazes me. He who is omniscient knew they would likely fail Him. Why didn't He select some flourishing empire such as China or India? Wouldn't they have been more likely to bring glory to His name?

The Lord told Moses that He chose them because He loved them (Deut. 7:8). Weakness seems to attract God. He who could see the end from the beginning knew that through this small nation He would best be able to display to the world His glory. History reveals the terrible flaws in the people God chose—it shows their willfulness, their arrogance and disobedience. But as we view His patience and love in dealing with them we observe a picture of God's mercy and justice that we could not otherwise see. The object lesson of ancient Israel enables us to believe that He will deal with present-day spiritual Israel with the same love and mercy.

"Christ can look upon the misery of the world without a shade of sorrow for having created man. In the human heart He sees more than sin, more than misery. In His infinite wisdom and love He sees man's possibilities, the height to which he may attain. He knows that, even though human beings have abused their mercies and destroyed their God-given dignity, yet the Creator is to be glorified in their redemption." [2]

But we must also remember that God will never ignore deliberate and willful sin. He does not look at us with blinders on. While He is fully aware of our sin, our impurity, He also knows what we can become through faith in Him. In Jeremiah 30 God rebukes the Israelites. "Your wound is incurable," He states in verse 12, "your injury beyond healing." Humanly speaking, they were hopeless. Yet a few verses later (verse 17) God makes the amazing promise: "But I will restore you to health and heal your wounds." *Now that is the power of God. Able to do the impossible, He can save the worst sinner. The Lord can heal our broken families and restore our churches to revival power.*

Jeremiah received a glorious promise:

26

> " 'This is the covenant I will make with the
> house of Israel
> after that time,' declares the Lord.
> 'I will put my law in their minds
> and write it on their hearts.
> I will be their God,
> and they will be my people.' "
>
> —Jeremiah 31:33

God wanted to write His laws in their hearts so that they would not only be able to obey His laws but would delight in doing so! But the majority refused. The author of Hebrews repeats the promise (Heb. 8:10), showing that God also meant it for the Christians, who were both Jews and Gentiles.

Jeremiah outlined the intimate covenant relationship that God wanted to have with His people: "They will be my people, and I will be their God. I will give them singleness of heart and action, so that they will always fear me for their own good and the good of their children after them. I will make an everlasting covenant with them: I will never stop doing good to them, and I will inspire them to fear me, so that they will never turn away from me" (Jer. 32:38-40).

How God longs for the love of His people!

So often we forget the marvelous love that He has for us. We doubt that it is really possible to have an intimate relationship with Him. And all the time God is standing close by, yearning and loving.

Every morning He calls to each of us, "Wake up! Wake up! Come talk with Me heart-to-heart in prayer. You share your heart and I'll share Mine." Our first waking thoughts should be of Him. The Bible clearly depicts God's love for individuals: children, lost sheep, sparrows—even demoniacs, murderers, and prodigals.

"The relations between God and *each soul* are as distinct and full as though there were not another soul . . . for whom He gave His beloved Son."[3]

---

[1] I am indebted to Jean Bartling for this illustration.

[2] Ellen G. White, *Thoughts From the Mount of Blessing* (Boise, Idaho: Pacific Press Pub. Assn., 1955), pp. vii, viii.

[3] White, *Steps to Christ* (Mountain View, Calif.: Pacific Press Pub. Assn., 1956), p.100. (Italics supplied.)

CHAPTER 2

## *His People Are a Royal Priesthood*

The Bible is a book written, not to hide God, but to reveal Him. Inspired Scripture reveals nothing but truth. The account of the Fall immediately follows the glorious story of Creation in the first two chapters of Genesis. Nowhere do Bible writers slant their messages just to make God look good. In fact, sometimes, humanly speaking, we wonder about the deity we read about in the Old Testament.

The story I would write if given the opportunity to let my imagination follow up the account of Creation would be totally unlike the true one. I'd make God look good by offering all sorts of explanations and defenses for Him as to why sin entered the garden. But the Lord has no need for anyone to protect Him. He has no desire to hide. Bare truth suffices for Him. In the long run it is what will lead us to Jesus and salvation. Truth fills every page of Scripture— often misunderstood but *always* there. The Holy Spirit will enable every honest seeker to find truth and put it together correctly to the glory of God, acknowledging, of course, that a human mind can never completely understand the Almighty. Throughout eternity we will be exploring the divine mind.

God never has to take back His words. When He entered into a covenant with Abraham, the promises He made to the patriarch and his descendants will last throughout eternity.

His promises do have conditions, however. Not because He isn't sure of what He says, but because He gives humanity free will. God makes this distinction very clear in His words. Speaking through the prophet Jeremiah, He says:

"If at any time I announce that a nation or kingdom is to be uprooted, torn down and destroyed, and if that nation I warned repents of its evil, then I will relent and not inflict on it the disaster I had planned. And if at another time I announce that a nation or kingdom is to be built up and planted, and if it does evil in my sight and does not obey me, then I will reconsider the good I had intended to do for it" (Jer. 18:7-10).

The same principle applies to individuals (Eze. 18:21-24).

Because God leaves human beings free to choose life or death, it may sometimes seem to us that His promises have failed—but they never do. God's side of the covenant never falters.

Not so with human promises. When God spoke the Ten Commandments in His own voice to the Israelites at Sinai, Scripture gives us an illustration of what human promises are like. What did the people say? "Everything the Lord has said we will do" (Ex. 24:3).

And what did they then do? They created the golden calf and worshiped it in place of God!

Moses recorded how God felt about their promise: "The Lord heard you when you spoke to me and the Lord said to me, 'I have heard what this people said to you. Everything they said was good'" (Deut. 5:28).

Their words were right. And their promise to obey was an honorable one.

But then God went on to show that He could read their

inner nature: "Oh, that their hearts would be inclined to fear me and keep all my commands always, so that it might go well with them and their children forever!" (verse 29).

They made their vow out of fear and not from their will. Because they refused to let God write His laws in their hearts, it was impossible for His chosen people to keep the beautiful agreement that He made with them. Their hardness of heart limited what they could do. For a covenant to be complete, there must be perfect promises on *both* sides. God's side was flawless, but the failure of His people to keep their promise shattered the covenant.

Yet He had a way prepared to complete both sides of the agreement—to make it a perfect whole. God the Son became a human being Himself, and His promises mesh perfectly with His Father's promises! We see God's face in the face of Jesus (2 Cor. 4:6)!

The New Testament describes it like this:

"But the ministry Jesus has received is as superior to theirs as the covenant of which he is mediator is superior to the old one, and it is founded on *better promises*. For if there had been nothing wrong with that first covenant, no place would have been sought for another. But God found fault with the people and said:

> 'The time is coming, declares the Lord,
>> when I will make a new covenant
> with the house of Israel
>> and with the house of Judah.
> It will not be like the covenant
>> I made with their forefathers
> when I took them by the hand
>> to lead them out of Egypt,
> because they did not remain faithful to my
>> covenant,

and I turned away from them, declares the
Lord.
This is the covenant I will make with the house
of Israel
after that time, declares the Lord.
I will put my laws in their minds
and write them on their hearts.
*I will be their God,*
*and they will be my people."*
—Hebrews 8:6-10

One of the most exciting things I discovered as I followed the thread of gold throughout Scripture, tracing God's yearning desire for intimacy with humanity, is that Jesus is on our side! Yes, He identifies with and supports the human race. He became a human being and will remain one with us throughout eternity! His promises can also be ours. Jesus is not only God but also one of the people, equally honored.

As I began this chapter I knew that the only way I could accurately discuss the great honor that God has bestowed upon us, as He joins us with His priestly ministry and work, was first to identify the Son of God as one of the people. When I read about the promises of Israel and their hearts not agreeing with the words they spoke, I realized that often I was like that too! My vows to obey God are no better than theirs. But Jesus, as a human being, said, "I always do what pleases [My Father]" (John 8:29). David prophesied of Him: "Then I said, 'Behold, I come; In the scroll of the book it is written of me. *I delight to do Your will, O my God, and Your law is within my heart"* (Ps. 40:7, 8, NKJV).

Here is God's will for each of us—His law written in our hearts. Because Jesus took our sins and died for us, He has made it possible for His law to be transcribed in each of our

32

hearts. Jesus still identifies Himself with us!

Through Moses God told His chosen people what His wonderful plan was for them: "Now if you obey me fully and keep my covenant, then out of all nations you will be my treasured possession. Although the whole earth is mine, you will be for me *a kingdom of priests and a holy nation"* (Ex. 19:5, 6).

"You will be a kingdom of priests," God said of His personally selected people.

But that puzzled me. You see, in the very next chapter of Exodus we read the awesome story of God speaking audibly to the vast company of freed slaves from the cloud-covered top of Mount Sinai. He not only proclaimed aloud the Ten Commandments, clearly stating the people's part of the agreement, but also engraved those commandments upon two stone tablets with His own fingers. Nowhere in all the pageantry surrounding the presence of God on Sinai did He mention the priesthood of this nation again.

In fact, the only other mention of priests that I found in Exodus involved God's instruction to Moses for building a house where He could dwell among His people. The Lord told Israel's leader to dedicate the entire tribe of Levi as priests to care for the ministry of His house. Moses spent a number of chapters detailing God's instructions as to the responsibilities of the Levite priests and even their attire, but nowhere could I again find any further mention of the entire nation as priests.

I'm afraid that I argued a bit with God as I contemplated all this. "I just can't understand why You say that everyone is to be a priest, and then You immediately select the tribe of Levi alone for that role. Didn't that confuse the people?" I asked.

It was then that He showed me something invaluable to

my growing Christian experience. *The services in the earthly sanctuary, whether the sacrifices or any of the rituals, never saved anyone.* God asked Moses to set up the sanctuary in the wilderness to illustrate the entire plan of salvation. Every sacrifice offered on the bronze altar represented the death of Jesus on the cross. And every article of furniture, every minute part of the service, acted as an illustration of how God was dealing with sin and sinners. The tabernacle itself depicted the heavenly sanctuary. The ritual of the high priest symbolized the work of mediation and intercession done in heaven by Jesus for sinners. The priesthood acted out the duties of the people of God! So the sanctuary services as a whole revealed God's face.

Thus the tribe of Levi was also only an *illustration* of the work that God was asking each individual to become involved in: worship of the true God, intercessory prayer ascending to heaven in behalf of others, loving service for humanity, and the teaching of righteousness. The sweet incense of the perfection of Jesus would accompany every personal prayer and empower every ministry of love.

Oh, I know, this was hundreds of years before Jesus became a human being and lived and died among humanity. But remember an important fact: the shadow of the cross fell backward as well as forward. Every person redeemed for eternity (past, present, and future) will be saved because of the death, resurrection, and intercession of Jesus Christ! The wilderness sanctuary modeled the heavenly sanctuary and the work of Jesus for our salvation—a visual picture of God's total and complete involvement with the human race.

So what was it that He expected of ancient Israel? Only this: He sought a people with His law written in their hearts, a people who would not only witness to the world

His righteous character, but who could also join Him in intercession for sinners! Yes, His people would be obedient—the Ten Commandments reveal the importance of obedience—but so much more than merely outwardly compliant. They would represent God here on earth as Jesus was representing them in heaven. It was God's plan for ancient Israel, and it is still His intention for His people today. We are to reveal the face of God to the world.

"Love for God, zeal for His glory, and love for fallen humanity, brought Jesus to earth to suffer and to die. This was the controlling power of His life. This principle He bids us adopt." [1]

When I began to understand the importance of the priesthood of God's chosen people I expected to find this subject again in the New Testament. And I was right! Both Peter and John, members of the inner circle of Christ's disciples, wrote about this important ministry of believers.

"As you come to him, the living Stone—rejected by men but chosen by God and precious to him—you also, like living stones, are being built into a spiritual house to be a *holy priesthood,* offering spiritual sacrifices acceptable to God through Jesus Christ" (1 Peter 2:4, 5).

In that same chapter Peter adds: "But you are a chosen people, *a royal priesthood, a holy nation,* a people belonging to God, that you may declare the praises of him who called you out of darkness into his wonderful light" (verse 9).

God is calling each of us today to join Jesus in His high priestly ministry of intercession. Not only are we to obey His laws, but also we are to actively participate with Christ in glorifying God in four areas of ministry: worship, intercessory prayer, loving service for humanity, and the teaching of righteousness.

We have no ability to do this except for the death, resurrection, and intercession of Jesus in our behalf and the marvelous infilling of the Holy Spirit to make Christ's gift come alive in us. But when we are Spirit-filled, we will actively participate with Jesus in the Most Holy Place of the heavenly sanctuary in intercession for sinners. One-on-one with God! What a privilege to join Jesus in His ministry![2]

The apostle John also speaks of the priesthood of believers. In the first chapter of Revelation he says: "To him who loves us and has freed us from our sins by his blood, and has made us to be *a kingdom and priests* to serve his God and Father—to him be glory and power for ever and ever! Amen" (Rev. 1:5, 6).

John's description of the throne room of heaven includes a thrilling passage about the 24 elders and the four living creatures as they fell on their faces before the Lamb of God. Each held a golden bowl full of incense (which, John explained, represented the prayers of the saints). The 24 elders and the four living creatures sang a new song of praise to the Lamb:

> "You are worthy to take the scroll
> and to open its seals,
> because you were slain,
> and with your blood you purchased men
> for God
> from every tribe and language and people and
> nation.
> You have made them to be *a kingdom
> and priests* to serve our God,
> and they will reign on the earth."
> —Revelation 5:9, 10

How clear this makes the message of the wilderness sanctuary! God planned all along to make His special chosen people coworkers with Him in revealing His glory to the world.

My husband and I recently participated in an inspiring 10-day camp meeting with the theme Worshiping the King. One of the speakers spoke on the topic of prayer. He quoted from Revelation, in which John describes another scene in heaven:

"Another angel, who had a golden censer, came and stood at the altar. He was given *much incense* to offer, with the prayers of all the saints, on the golden altar before the throne. The smoke of the incense, together with the prayers of the saints, went up before God from the angel's hand" (Rev. 8:3, 4).

The presenter went on to explain that God takes our small, weak prayers and adds to them His *"much incense"*—the powerful prayers of Jesus Himself! A human prayer is never offered up to God alone but always accompanied by the *"much incense"* of Jesus' prayers.

The Lord selected very carefully even the land He promised to Abraham as the home of His chosen people. Not only was it a land described in Scripture as "flowing with milk and honey," a land where produce flourished abundantly, but it was also on the main trade route of the nations of that day.

God's plan was that His people would be witnesses—to reveal His face—to those who passed through Israel. His Temple, He said, was to be a house of prayer for *all* people. No one was to be excluded.

It was never His plan that His truth would be shut up among His people only. Truth hidden deliberately from the ignorant soon diminishes. God's chosen people—as a whole and as individuals—were to illustrate to the world divine glory, and by their love and tender concern for the aliens among them, they were to become teachers of truth.

Even the times when God found it necessary to discipline His people through drought and famine, through wars and exile, His purpose for His people steadily continued to unfold. They were to have exemplary lives before the nations among whom they were exiled. We read about the little servant girl in Elisha's time, of Ezra, Nehemiah, Daniel, and his friends in Babylon—what opportunities they all had to witness to the power of the true God within a pagan realm!

One of my favorite Bible narratives is a familiar one. You remember the story of Ruth, the young woman in the land of Moab who married a Jewish man whose family had fled there to escape a terrible famine in Israel. Her father-in-law, her husband, and her husband's brother all died tragically in Moab. Naomi, the mother-in-law, decided it was time to return to her homeland. She easily persuaded the other daughter-in-law, Orpah, to stay in Moab with her own family. But the life of her mother-in-law had attracted Ruth. She saw in Naomi's God someone wholly unlike the often cruel deities of her people.

"Don't urge me to leave you," Ruth told Naomi. "Where you go I will go, and where you stay I will stay. *Your people will be my people and your God my God"* (Ruth 1:16).

God had planned that His chosen people would attract the honest-hearted seekers of truth in every nation. By this means the whole world would come to know Him. Many of the people whom God displaced in order to give their land to Israel had once known the true Lord. For many years Abraham and his descendants lived only as homeless pilgrims in tents in Canaan, the land that God promised him would one day belong to his descendants as their inheritance, while the Lord dealt patiently with the existing nations.

Melchizedek, king of the city of Salem (as people called

38

Jerusalem in those days), was a priest of the Most High God, and Abraham paid tithes to him. But through the ensuing generations constant contact with wickedness extinguished the knowledge of the true God in Melchizedek's land, and the Lord finally turned it over to the descendants of Abraham, the children of Israel.

God did not completely destroy any nation until it had filled the cup of its own iniquity. Throughout the known world countless individuals still sought truth. It was the privilege of God's people to reach such persons for Him. His face shows clearly through the priesthood of believers.

Jesus, our example, demonstrated for us how to do it. The people of Samaria, although looked down upon by the Jews, were important to Him, and His missionary journeys often included the cities of Samaria. The Greek woman in the area of Tyre received the great blessing of healing for her demon-possessed daughter. Jesus healed the demoniacs of Gadara and fed the 4,000. He welcomed the questions of the Greeks who sought Him in the Temple just before His crucifixion.

I wish I could properly put into words the joy it brings me as I realize that the golden theme of intimacy between God and humanity throughout the Bible includes *me*. God so loved me that He gave His beloved Son to live and die and live again to redeem *my* life. Through my faith in Jesus God became *my* God, and I became one of His people.

Scripture repeats the theme "I will be your God and you will be My people" again and again. Whenever God says "My people" or the prophets declare "My God," you know Scripture has in mind the golden thread of intimacy between God and the human race in His everlasting covenant. His people are to clearly display His face in the world.

King David put it into words of prayer: "You have established your people Israel as your *very own* forever, and you, O Lord, have become their God" (2 Sam. 7:24).

Through David's son Solomon we hear God's heart cry: "If my people, who are called by my name, will humble themselves and pray and seek my face and turn from their wicked ways, then will I hear from heaven and will forgive their sin and will heal their land" (2 Chron. 7:14).

The apostle John ties it all together in the final book of the Bible: "And I heard a loud voice from the throne saying, 'Now the dwelling of God is with men, and he will live with them. They will be his people, and God himself will be with them and be their God'" (Rev. 21:3).

Praise God! We are His people, His partners in ministry, for all eternity.

### The Face of God

### in

### "I Am Your God and You Are My People"

When God says, "I am your God and you are My people," we see a deity whose face remains continually turned toward earth and the human beings He created to live here. The eternal God who dwells in a high and holy place lost His heart to His creation. After the majority of humanity rebelled against Him, He chose one man, faithful Abraham, and promised him that through his descendants the world would be turned right again.

Throughout Scripture we find God repeating again and again the very same covenant of love that He made to Adam and Eve in Eden. Noah, Enoch, Abraham, Isaac, Jacob, Moses, David, Daniel, and others like them—and finally the

Son of God Himself—lived out before the world aspects of the covenant response that God so desired from all His created beings.

We see God in person in Jesus Christ while He was a human being like ourselves. How impossible—but true! When we see the life Jesus exhibited as a human being, we long to live like that too. We see His patience in training the 12 disciples to become His representatives—His priests in worship, intercession, service, teaching—and learn that we too are to be priests in the same type of ministry. Then when the leadership of the people He first chose to reveal His character to the world rebelled, He renewed His everlasting covenant to the worldwide Christian church—same promises, same joyful reality.

Throughout Scripture we see a triune God who wants to live in us and invites us to live in Him. He wants to walk every step of our pathway with us, talk with us daily. The life and death of Jesus guarantees that everyone who chooses eternal life can have it.

---

[1] Ellen G. White, *The Desire of Ages* (Mountain View, Calif.: Pacific Press Pub. Assn., 1898), p. 330.

[2] Read more about the ministry of intercession in my book *When We Pray for Others* (Hagerstown, Md.: Review and Herald Pub. Assn., 1995).

## PART II

## *"I Am Your Father and You Are My Child"*

Our Father in heaven,
hallowed be your name,
your kingdom come,
your will be done
on earth as it is in heaven.
Give us today our daily bread.
Forgive us our debts,
as we also have forgiven our debtors.
And lead us not into temptation,
but deliver us from the evil one."

—Matthew 6:9-13

CHAPTER 3

## *The Loving Father*

Perhaps the most heartwarming face of God we see in Scripture is that of the Father. In the past two chapters we have observed the Almighty as a leader of a chosen people. We have witnessed His power and His glory as He works astounding miracles, shouts from a mountaintop, appears in a pillar of fire. Scripture depicts Him as ruler, lawgiver, one who exacts obedience. But we also have caught a glimpse of Him as a God who wants to be intimate with humanity, who chose a people to be His very own.

And now, as the Father, God takes on a human face. God knew that sinful humanity would find it difficult to picture a high and holy God. So throughout Scripture the Holy Spirit clearly outlines for us the many faces of God—the many visible links we can find to Him in our human relationships and in the world of nature. Though no human words can perfectly describe Him, yet we can hear His plaintive call throughout Scripture as the Holy Spirit describes in various ways the intimate relationship God longs to have with us. We find the stirring of a growing hope that it is really possible to know God better than we do even our closest human friend.

What is God as a Father like?

"As a father has compassion on his children, so the Lord

has compassion on those who fear him" (Ps. 103:13).

Matthew, Mark, Luke, and John give us the clearest picture of God found in the Bible. John declares that "no one has seen God at any time. The only begotten Son, who is in the bosom of the Father, He has declared Him" (John 1:18, NKJV).

Jesus is the only God human beings have seen with physical eyes. Prophecy says of the coming Redeemer:

"For to us a child is born,

to us a son is given,

and the government will be on his shoulders.

And he will be called

Wonderful Counselor, Mighty God,

*Everlasting Father,* Prince of Peace."

—Isaiah 9:6

Jesus as a part of the triune God exhibits the same characteristics as the other Two. In character and power They are all three the same. The human face that Jesus revealed to the people around Him was also the face of the Father God.

Because of the weakness or wickedness of some human fathers the idea of God's being a Father is often difficult to carry over from our intellect into our emotions. But as we see the relationship of God the Father and God the Son lived out in the New Testament, this Bible picture comes alive for us.

Few of us have had ideal fathers. If we think of God as being like the man we called Daddy, we may find ourselves severely hampered in understanding this important face of God. But God does not ask us to pattern Him after our fathers—even the best of human fathers. No, instead He shows us the Father who is everything we ever dreamed of in a father—and more!

A few years ago I read a book written by a woman who

simply called herself "Esther's Child," after the fatherless Esther in the Bible story. The author grew up in a dysfunctional home with an uncaring mother and an abusive father. From an early age she felt she had no protection except what she gave herself. When she was a teenager, she discovered God, and in the church she found the loving family she did not have. But when she married a man who professed to be a Christian, the marriage led only to more abuse.

Several failed marriages later she felt she was losing even her church family. Surely, the people contended, a virtuous woman would not find herself in a bad marriage more than once. Their criticisms stabbing to the very depths of her heart, she longed for an earthly father who would stand up for her and put her accusers on the run.

Her two little children and her personal relationship with God were all that she had left. And she worried that she was losing God. She felt that all she had ever brought Him throughout her short life was reproach. Had He forsaken her? Also she feared for the lives of her children and herself in her present marriage.

"If You have not completely forsaken me, Lord," she prayed, "please reveal Yourself to me."

Early the next morning she opened her Bible and began to read Psalms. To her amazement Psalm 18 revealed the Father she had always longed for! She found described there a Father who out of His love for her reached down and took hold of her and rescued her from her enemies. Psalm 18 depicted a deity who promised to bring her to a place where no one could condemn her. All this because He delighted in her!

She rejoiced in the idea of God as a Father-protector. But immediately she began to doubt. Could it possibly be true? Was God really speaking to her through Scripture?

Could she count on Psalm 18 as being a special message to her from God? Her own unwise decisions had gotten her in this mess. She did not feel worthy to have God speak to her. But without Him she had no one to protect or rescue her. Reluctantly she gave the glorious promise of Psalm 18 back to the Lord.

But the memory of her delight at the revelation of a Father-protector would not leave her. Just in case it had really been God speaking to her, she begged Him to give her the same message in some other way. If she received the thought a second time, perhaps she could have faith enough to believe that God would really be her protector.

The next day as she opened her Bible for guidance her eyes caught familiar words in an unfamiliar place. Although her Bible was now open to 2 Samuel, the words she discovered there were identical to those she had read the day before in Psalm 18! Yes, it was Psalm 18 all over again, but this time recorded in 2 Samuel 22. God had answered her prayer. He had given her the exact message of hope and love once more. Surely she could trust a deity such as that to lead her out of the nightmare her life had become. God was truly the Father she had always longed for.*

Although the Old Testament has numerous references comparing God to a father—or even a mother—nowhere do any of the Old Testament prayers begin with the words "My Father." Scripture seems to apply the term *father* to God only as an illustration or contrast. Yet the message of the Old Testament is clear. God was always a loving Father to His people: "A father to the fatherless, a defender of widows, is God in his holy dwelling" (Ps. 68:5).

> "How gladly would I treat you like sons
> and give you a desirable land,
> the most beautiful inheritance of any nation.

I thought you would call me 'Father'
    and not turn away from following me."
                        —Jeremiah 3:19

"Can a mother forget the baby at her breast
    and have no compassion on the child she
        has borne?
Though she may forget,
    I will not forget you!
See, I have engraved you on the palms of my
        hands;
    your walls are ever before me."
                    —Isaiah 49:15, 16

It's almost as though the believers in the Old Testament felt that they could *liken* God to a loving father or mother, or *contrast* Him with an earthly parent. But it seemed beyond their understanding to actually *call* Him Father.

And most likely that is true. Because of the great disparity between most human parents and God, how can anyone picture Him as a Father? God gives us the perfect picture in the New Testament! The relationship between God the Father and God the Son is perfect. Here we find the Father who will always protect, always love. No wonder the patriarchs could not call Him Father. They had never witnessed a perfect father-child relationship. *But we have—we've seen Jesus with His Father.*

Jesus taught His followers to call God Father. And then He went ahead and showed them *how* to talk with God as their heavenly Father by praying with them a simple model prayer. And through His recorded words we can begin to catch a glimpse of the things God is interested in as our Father. Because Jesus spent time daily in prayer with His Father, the disciples saw firsthand the intimacy between the Father and the Son. They began to sense the glorious relationship of a Father God with His children. It was beyond their wildest dream and greatest hope.

Large crowds followed Jesus wherever He went: the sick in need of healing, the hungry craving food, the poor looking for wealth, the rich wanting power—and yes, some honest in heart seeking a Savior. As He faced the muttering of the quarrelsome multitude how He longed for each of them to know His Father as their Father too!

"There was a man who had two sons," Jesus began. The crowd quieted. He was a great storyteller, and they hung on His words.

"The younger son said to his father, 'Father, give me my share of the estate.'" Thus Jesus began the story that we know today as the parable of the prodigal son. But had Jesus named it, He might well have called it the parable of the waiting father. For the story centers not on the rebellious son, but on the Fatherhood of God.

God is our Father! No matter if our human father couldn't love us—or if he even abused us. We, who feel so unworthy, so unlovable, are dearly loved by the King of the universe. His love is lavish, unstinting, never ending. As we bask in that love we begin to realize how important it is to do what pleases Him—not to gain His love, but because we already have it.

Paul describes this relationship. "Those who are led by the Spirit of God are sons of God," the apostle reminds his readers. "For you did not receive a spirit that makes you a slave again to fear, but you received the Spirit of sonship. And by him we cry, 'Abba, Father.' The Spirit Himself testifies with our spirit that we are God's children. Now if we are children, then we are heirs—heirs of God and co-heirs with Christ, if indeed we share in his sufferings in order that we may also share in his glory" (Rom. 8:14-17).

On the Father's side we see His mercy, compassion, and love for His children, His personal interest in us, and His willingness to provide not only for our every need but also for our protection. When we enter into relationship with God, we show ourselves willing to love, honor, and respect Him as our Father. We acknowledge our dependence upon Him, our confidence in His judgment, His integrity, and His abilities. As a result we seek to obey His will and accept His discipline and guidance.

I love watching through Scripture the way God the Son lived out this relationship with His Father, the way He spontaneously spoke of His love for the Father and the Father's love for Him. The religious leaders couldn't handle it! Not a one of them would have dared to familiarly call God Father. Instead they referred to Him as "the Lord Almighty," "the Holy One," "Sovereign of the world," or some other exalted title. When they could not curb Christ's tongue, they sought to take His life. How dare this illegitimate man from Nazareth claim God as His Father (John 5:17, 18)!

Sometimes Jesus broke into prayer right in the middle of a conversation with others. Just after He rode into Jerusalem on a donkey with the people cheering Him all the way, hailing Him as king of Israel, He went to the Temple to teach the people for the last time. To His disciples it seemed that the tide was turning in their favor. They assumed that Jesus would soon set up His earthly kingdom. But He Himself knew His time was short, and His heart was heavy at the thought of the inevitable separation from His Father that awaited Him. In His humanity He did not see how He could bear it. Yet because He had willingly taken upon Himself the sins of the world, it was necessary. Sin is so offensive to God that the sense of His Father's presence could not remain with Him as He died the death of the sinner. He must perish alone.

Sorrow now engulfed Him. Putting aside His sadness, He proclaimed the word of truth to anyone in the Temple who would listen. Philip and Andrew came into the inner part of the Temple where Jesus was teaching to tell Him that a group of Greeks in the outer court were asking to see Him. As always, Jesus responded to the heart cry "We would see Jesus!" When He spoke with the delegation from Greece, His heart rejoiced as He realized that it was only a foreshadowing of how the gospel would spread throughout the world because of His life-and-death mission.

Again sorrow overtook Him as He spoke to the Greeks, and He openly admitted His heartache. "Now my heart is troubled, and what shall I say? 'Father, save me from this hour'? No, it was for this very reason I came to this hour" (John 12:27).

At that point He broke into prayer, speaking only to His Father.

"Father," He requested, 'glorify your name!" (verse 28).

A voice responded from heaven.

" 'I have glorified it, and will glorify it again,' " the Father said. "The crowd that was there and heard it said it had thundered; others said an angel had spoken to him" (verses 28, 29).

The Son of God had glorified the Father's name throughout His life and would do so, even more magnificently, as He died on the cross the death that humanity deserved, thus making eternal life possible for all who would accept it. What's more, God the Father knew that because of Jesus' life and death the name of God would be glorified again and again by His faithful children throughout the ages. With love and pity the Father spoke assurance to His beloved Son.

That day in the Temple as He spoke to the Greeks was the last of the three times the Bible records that the Father spoke audibly with His Son. The first was at His baptism, the second on the Mount of Transfiguration.

As the voice of God died away in the Temple courtyard Jesus spoke again to the people.

"This voice was for your benefit, not mine," He said (verse 30). As always, His faith in His Father was so complete that He did not need to hear an audible voice to believe in Him. Even though Jesus was the Son of God, He most often heard His Father speak to Him through the inward voice of the Holy Spirit, just as the rest of us do. The inner presence was enough for Jesus.

Truly the life of His Son had glorified the Father. And through Jesus' death and resurrection God would be glorified again. And again. And again throughout all earth time.

Truly Jesus has revealed the Father to us, and now we too can call Him Father.

---

* Esther's Child, *Light Through the Dark Glass* (Boise, Idaho: Pacific Press Pub. Assn., 1988).

## CHAPTER 4

## *Sons and Daughters of God*

"How great is the love the Father has lavished on us,
that we should be called children of God!" (1 John 3:1).

As a girl I dearly loved my dolls but enjoyed babies only from afar. The summer I was 13, though, my mother arranged for me to baby-sit two little neighbor boys while their mother worked. The very first day the boys recognized me as a frightened novice and refused to obey me. On the second day they ran away, and I raced home crying to my mother. That was the end of my baby-sitting career!

But when I fell in love and married, I began to look at babies and children in a new way. I could hardly wait to have children born as the fruit of my husband's and my love. Children who would call me "Mommy" and my husband "Daddy."

John and I surprised our families by giving birth to four children in four years and three months! I would have welcomed a dozen children, but reason limited our family to four. For years, whenever I saw a baby, my arms ached to hold another precious little life of my very own. I felt that motherhood was my calling. My mother told me later that for several years she feared I would never again be able to carry on an adult conversation about any other subject than babies!

Often human beings selfishly have children to satisfy their own needs, but God created His human children so that He could delight in their fellowship and lavish His love upon them. How He loves to love!

God always gives us the choice of being born into His family. As human babies we came into the world through someone else's decision. But God patiently calls us, woos us, and when we turn and seek Him, He eagerly accepts us into His family. "To all who received him, to those who believed in his name, he gave the right to become children of God—children born not of natural descent, nor of human decision or a husband's will, but born of God" (John 1:12, 13).

The lavishness of the love of God our Father is difficult for human beings to understand. We want things to be reasonable. And there is no reasonable explanation as to why God loves such unlovable creatures as sinners. He alone exemplifies the perfect blend of mercy and justice. And love is the center of both that mercy and justice.

One morning I read the Ten Commandments during my devotional time.

"Father," I requested, "I know the Ten Commandments so well. I've even memorized them in more than one version. But please help me to see a new picture of You in them this morning. Show me something I haven't noticed before."

I found it in the second commandment. God says that He punishes the children for the sins of the fathers to the third and fourth generation of those who hate Him. In the version I was reading, the rest of that passage is: "But showing love to a thousand generations of those who love me and keep my commandments" (Ex. 20:6). Suddenly I realized the great contrast between His punishment and His love: His punishment is spare—He chastises exactly as much as is necessary to eradicate sin from the universe for all time. No extra retribution for good measure—just exactly what is necessary. But how different with His love! He pours it out lavishly.

Let me illustrate this from life: My husband likes plenty of syrup with his pancakes. Sometimes when he orders a stack of pancakes at a restaurant, the server brings just one small plastic container of syrup, barely enough to spread over the top of one pancake. But other times he or she will arrive with a whole pitcher of syrup that John can pour over the entire stack of pancakes until it drips over onto the plate—just the way he likes it! That's God's love for His children. With no limit to it, He lets it drip all over the place—even onto those who do not love Him in return!

In a certain sense all human beings are God's children. God is the Creator of all life. Scripture also calls the created beings on the other inhabited worlds and the angels the sons of God (see Job 1:6, NKJV). But after Adam and Eve sinned, He bought humanity back from the enemy by the death of His Son. He is *twice* our Father!

The New Testament refers to Jesus as the only begotten of the Father when He was given to our world (John 3:16). After His death and resurrection His title changed. He became the firstborn over all creation (Col. 1:15). Jesus is no longer an only child, but the first of a whole family of children! All humanity became His younger brothers and sisters. We can all call God Father. The Lord finally has the large and secure family that He has always wanted—secured by the blood of Jesus!

In another sense we can describe all of God's "born again" children as "firstborn sons." Patriarchal times placed great importance upon the birthright that passed down from father to oldest son. The firstborn son not only received the larger share of land and livestock but also became priest of the family and was believed to receive special blessings from God for the responsibility. In the biblical story of twins Esau and Jacob, the firstborn, Esau, scorned the priesthood and sold his birthright to his younger brother, Jacob, who especially coveted the spiritual blessing.

Early in the Bible God introduced the symbol of the firstborn. In Exodus God sent Moses to lead His chosen people out of slavery, only to encounter an obstinate Pharaoh who refused to let the people go. God demonstrated His power through a series of plagues upon the land and people of Egypt, always protecting His own children from harm. The final plague was the strongest yet.

"If you do not let My people go," God said through Moses, "I will slay all the firstborn in Egypt, both people and animals." "Except," God added, "in every house of My people where the blood of the slain lamb is brushed upon the doorpost, I will preserve the firstborn" (dialogue paraphrased from Exodus 11; 12). As the death angel slew the firstborn of the Egyptians he passed over every home of the Hebrews where the blood of a lamb had been smeared on the doorpost.

The blood of a lamb has since Eden represented the necessity of the death of a Redeemer to save humanity from sin. At Sinai God symbolically transferred the priestly ministry from the firstborn child of each family to the entire tribe of Levi as an illustration of His desire for all of us. In the days of the apostles God made it clear that the special birthright blessing of being a priest involved all believers. The Levitical priesthood had depicted the service God seeks from all His children. Hundreds of years later the real Passover Lamb was crucified as the priest politicians blindly performed the familiar Passover rituals.

God longs for obedient children, those who will return

His love and call Him Father. And He finds them in those who hear His voice, repent of their sins, and are baptized into the family of God. The Bible tells us that the Lord even keeps a special book, the book of life, listing the names of all His born-again children.

Through our human mothers we can understand much about God as a father. Think of how a mother's eyes light up in the presence of her children. She cherishes each small token of their favor.

I remember my second son in his babyhood often stopping in his play to smile sweetly at me, saying, "Me loves you, Mommy." I still cherish that memory!

A mother is like that. And God is like that too. Mothers keep baby books to remember a child's growth and accomplishments. God maintains them too:

"Then those who feared the Lord talked with each other, and the Lord listened and heard. A scroll of remembrance was written in his presence concerning those who feared the Lord and honored his name. 'They will be mine,' says the Lord Almighty, 'in the day when I make up my treasured possession. I will spare them, just as in compassion a man spares his son who serves him'" (Mal. 3:16, 17).

The Old Testament promises are not just for the Israelites. They are also for you and me, as the apostle Paul makes very clear: "You are all sons of God through faith in Christ Jesus, for all of you who were baptized into Christ have clothed yourselves with Christ. There is neither Jew nor Greek, slave nor free, male nor female, for you are all one in Christ Jesus. If you belong to Christ, then you are Abraham's seed, and heirs according to the promise" (Gal. 3:26-29).

Notice that this passage blends Jews and Greeks, slave and free, male and female. In Jesus we are all God's firstborn children, another illustration of the same truth we found in the priesthood of all believers. As women we can accept this promise as readily as men can. God is not partial.

Let me give you a personal example of what this means in our lives and our relationship with God.

One morning I woke up hating myself. I had failed God so miserably the day before that I doubted even God's ability to make anything worthwhile out of me. When I am in the throes of self-hatred or depression, physical activity seems the only cure. So I decided it was the day to clean the grout on my kitchen counters. With a feeling of gloom I got out the cleanser, bleach, and scrub brush, and set to work. As I scrubbed with all my might I unconsciously began to pray.

"I'm hopeless, Lord," I cried. "I fail You again and again in the same ways. I never seem to learn." The more hopeless I felt, the harder I scrubbed.

"O Lord," I sobbed in resignation, "whatever do You think of me?"

At the time I didn't realize that I was praying, so I was surprised to hear God answer me.

"Carrol," He said, "you are My beloved daughter, in whom I am well pleased."

It was as though the sun came out from behind a dark cloud. Joy leaped up in my heart. I scrubbed even harder but this time with unspeakable peace. God loved me, understood me; I was His beloved daughter, and He forgave me and would help me overcome.

I knew God wasn't pleased with my failure the day before—but He was pleased at my repentance—my turning to Him in my distress.

"The word that was spoken to Jesus at the Jordan, 'This is My beloved Son, in whom I am well pleased,' embraces humanity. God spoke to Jesus as our representative. With all our sins and weaknesses, we are not cast aside as worthless. . . . The glory that rested upon Christ is a pledge of the love of God for us. It tells us of the power of prayer—how the human voice may reach the ear of God, and our petitions find acceptance in the courts of heaven. By sin, earth was cut off from heaven, and alienated from its communion; but Jesus has connected it again with the sphere of glory. His love has encircled man, and reached the highest heaven. The light which fell from the open portals upon the head of our Saviour will fall upon us as we pray for help to resist temptation. The voice which spoke to Jesus says to every believing soul, This is My beloved child, in whom I am well pleased."*

How wonderful to be a child of God!

The apostle Paul tells us: "But when the time had fully come, God sent his Son, born of a woman, born under law, to redeem those under law, that we might receive the full rights of sons. Because you are sons, God sent the Spirit of his Son into our hearts, the Spirit who calls out, 'Abba, Father.' So you are no longer a slave, but a son; and since you are a son, God has made you also an heir" (Gal. 4:4-7).

Paul mentions here the Holy Spirit as being the one who teaches us to call out, "Abba, Father." It is the Holy Spirit who helps us understand and communicate with God. Although each member of the Godhead has His own individual role, yet the entire fullness of the Godhead is present in each of Them.

Paul says of Jesus, "God was pleased to have all his fullness dwell in him" (Col. 1:19). We already know that all the totality of God was in the Father. It stands to reason that within the third member of the Godhead would also be all the fullness of God. Each has the same mind, thinks the same thoughts. But each plays a different role in salvation. The beautiful characteristics of motherhood, which we think of as feminine, are actually a part of God's image implanted largely in the female of our species and to a smaller extent in the male. These characteristics derive from the entire Godhead: Father, Son, and Holy Spirit. God is a mother as well as a father!

Jesus promised His followers before His death that when He left them He would send the Holy Spirit to take His place here on earth. Although the Holy Spirit had been active throughout biblical times, people never clearly understood His role until Jesus revealed both the Father and the Holy Spirit. With the life and death of Jesus as the basis of His mission the Holy Spirit was able to work in might and power.

The apostle Paul tells us that when a person first believes on Christ, he or she receives a "deposit" of the Holy Spirit, "guaranteeing what is to come" (2 Cor. 1:22; cf. Eph. 1:13, 14). But it is God's plan to give us more—much more than just a deposit—of the Spirit if we will only ask! We can be filled daily. Christ assures us of the willingness of the Godhead to give the Holy Spirit to all who request. We never need be without the mighty gift of the Spirit. In fact, Jesus combines this promise with the Fatherhood of God:

"Which of you fathers, if your son asks for a fish, will give him a snake instead? Or if he asks for an egg, will give him a scorpion? If you then, though you are evil, know how to give good gifts to your children, how much more will your Father in heaven give the Holy Spirit to those who ask Him!" (Luke 11:11-13).

Two great Old Testament promises help us to understand the plans that God has for His children through the third member of the Godhead, the Holy Spirit. The prophet Isaiah, writing under the inspiration of the Holy Spirit, tells us how the Son of God was able to live a sinless, holy life as a human being:

"A shoot will come up from the stump of Jesse;
　　from his roots a Branch [Jesus] will bear fruit.
The Spirit of the Lord will rest on him—
　　the Spirit of wisdom and of understanding,
　　the Spirit of counsel and of power,
　　the Spirit of knowledge and of the fear of the
　　　Lord—
and he will delight in the fear of the Lord.
He will not judge by what he sees with his eyes,
　　or decide by what he hears with his ears;
but with righteousness he will judge the needy,
　　with justice he will give decisions for the poor
　　　of the earth.
He will strike the earth with the rod of his mouth;
　　with the breath of his lips he will slay the wicked.
Righteousness will be his belt
　　and faithfulness the sash around his waist."

　　　　　　　　　　　　　　　　—Isaiah 11:1-5

Here we see perfectly described the ways that God the Father and God the Holy Spirit enabled God the Son to live a totally sinless human life. The amazing truth is that our Father is willing to do the same for His earthly children! In fact, it is only by the indwelling Spirit that humanity is ever able to overcome sin.

The second promise also comes from Isaiah and is one that God led me to years ago to encourage me in my daily prayer life. In this verse God the Son is speaking, and He is telling how it will be possible each day as a human being for Him to understand clearly the will of His Father and to have just the right words to speak to the people:

　　"The Sovereign Lord has given me an instructed
　　　tongue,
　　　to know the word that sustains the weary.

He wakens me morning by morning,
>   wakens my ear to listen like one being taught."
>                                           —Isaiah 50:4

Although the passage does not mention the Holy Spirit by name, we know that the inward voice of God is always the Holy Spirit—and it was this voice that Jesus constantly heard. It encourages us to realize that He learned just as we do, that God called Him every morning to instruct Him. The Lord will summon us in the same way if we but ask. What a privilege it is to be sons and daughters of God! God's children are heirs to His riches:

"Dear friends, now we are children of God, and what we will be has not yet been made known. But we know that when he appears, we shall be like him, for we shall see him as he is. Everyone who has this hope in him purifies himself, just as he is pure" (1 John 32, 3).

In the last book of the Bible the apostle John describes the final scene of victory, the New Jerusalem descending from heaven to earth, as God makes His triumphal third entry to our planet, accompanied by all the redeemed. The work of redemption has concluded. A newly cleansed and recreated earth is the heritage of God's children. "He who overcomes will inherit all this, and I will be his God and he will be my son" (Rev. 21:7).

The Face of God

in

"I Am Your Father and You Are My Child"

Perhaps the closest we come here on earth to seeing

the face of God is a mother or father bending over their child, their face lit up with love. The Old Testament Scriptures portray the majesty of God, high and holy, yet they also give us glimpses of the Lord's tender side: "As a father has compassion on his children, so the Lord has compassion on those who fear Him" (Ps. 103:13). "As a mother comforts her child, so will I comfort you" (Isa. 66:13).

But the New Testament reveals Him as the Father of our beloved Jesus—and the love between Jesus and His Father draws us to the Father too. Jesus taught us to pray, "Our Father which art in heaven." When we accept Jesus as our Savior from sin, God is our Father too.

Although our human father may have been vindictive, abusive, or so wounded himself that he was unable to give us the love and discipline we needed, our heavenly Father fulfills our wildest dream of what a perfect parent should be.

God is the ideal Father: His love is unconditional—He loves us even when we are the least lovely. He is always with us—guiding, guarding. Faithful in discipline, He helps us to mature in our Christian life. Not only is He our protector from evil, in the world and in our hearts, but He is always ready to listen to our recitation of complaints—our sorrows, our pain, our needs. And He rejoices when we rush to Him with our joys and admiration.

For ever and ever He will be our Father.

---

\* E. G. White, *The Desire of Ages,* p. 113.

PART III

## *"I Am Your Husband and You Are My Wife"*

For your Maker is your husband—
the Lord Almighty is his name—
the Holy One of Israel is your Redeemer;
he is called the God of all the earth."

—Isaiah 54:5

" 'Return, faithless people,' declares the Lord,
'for I am your husband.' "

—Jeremiah 3:14

" 'Like a woman unfaithful to her husband,
so you have been unfaithful to me, O house of Israel,'
declares the Lord."

—Jeremiah 3:20

"As a bridegroom rejoices over his bride,
so will your God rejoice over you."

—Isaiah 62:5

## CHAPTER 5

## *The Case of the Beguiled Prophet*

Hosea, son of Beeri, had early sensed the call of God upon his life. He never dreamed the great destiny that God had in mind for his ministry—that the messages the Lord gave him would touch the lives of four kings of Judah and one king in Israel. But the biggest amazement of all to Hosea would have been to realize that the intimacy of his marriage would become public knowledge and that his Spirit-led home life would be a constant series of heartbreak, forgiveness, and disappointment. The prophet never dreamed that his story would touch the lives of millions of people throughout earth time or that his life record revealed to the universe victories where he saw failure.

Imagine God asking a young minister today to marry a known prostitute! Yet that was exactly the Lord's message to Hosea. Surely it must have stunned him. He had lived a life of purity, avoiding anything that would separate him from God. As with Job, he could say, "I made a covenant with my eyes not to look lustfully at a girl" (Job 31:1). When Hosea considered marriage, it was with a godly virgin in mind.

"Surely this isn't Your voice, Lord," I can imagine him remonstrating with God. "I have no desire for a sinful woman. This union would dishonor Your name and end any usefulness I could have in Your service. Please tell me that You are only testing me as You did Abraham when You asked him to sacrifice his promised son!"

But no voice released Hosea from the divine command. He found no lamb caught in the thicket. Hosea could do nothing but say, "Not my will, Lord, but Yours be done."

As soon as Hosea took the first step in obedience God gave him the ability to look beyond the gaudy beauty of Gomer, to see deep into her heart and discover the helpless, homeless, fearful child masquerading as a bold temptress.

And so our pure young prophet fell in love! Deeply in love. Not with her beauty of face and form—though as a man Hosea no doubt responded to and delighted in her femininity. But the love God gave him for Gomer reflected the Lord's love for His people. It was a divine love, a love seldom encountered upon earth. And the heartache and grief Hosea endured throughout his marriage echoed God's heartache over His adulterous people.

In no other way could the Lord have more accurately and dramatically expressed His sorrow over Israel's infidelity than through this pageant of betrayed trust. As we read the story of Hosea we find ourselves amazed at the divine long-suffering and God's endless forgiveness. We see into the intricacies of His dealings with sinners and are encouraged to believe that hope also exists for us.

And we find answers to our questions. For example, what does God do when we willfully turn away from Him for other lovers? Does He leave us in disgust and anger?

In the book of Hosea God tells us His strategies for protecting His wayward lover:

> "Therefore I will block her path with thornbushes;
> I will wall her in so that she cannot find her way.
> She will chase after her lovers but not catch them;
> she will look for them but not find them.

Then she will say,
'I will go back to my husband as at first,
    for then I was better off than now.'"

—Hosea 2:6, 7

When I discovered these verses, I began to see how God uses His gentle force of love to make sin hard, distasteful, and unfulfilling. Since then I have often asked Him to put thornbushes around my children to protect them from falling into the evils of the world. I believe that God delights to have us join Him in praying the same prayers that Jesus, our High Priest, does. Such intercessory prayers are part of the service that God asks us, as priests, to offer in behalf of our families.

As God makes sin distasteful and hard, He also actively seeks us:

"Therefore I am now going to allure her;
    I will lead her into the desert
    and speak tenderly to her.
There I will give her back her vineyards,
        and will make the Valley of Achor* a door
        of hope."

—Hosea 2:14, 15

Trouble equals hope? How can that be? The concept reminds me of what James had to say: "Consider it pure joy, my brothers, whenever you face trials of many kinds, because you know that the testing of your faith develops perseverance. Perseverance must finish its work so that you may be mature and complete, not lacking anything" (James 1:2-4).

Joyful in trouble? I hope Hosea experienced it—the joy of knowing that God was leading in his relationship with Gomer.

Even the children she bore could not seem to hold her in her marriage commitment. In His first instruction to

Hosea God specified that he would not only have an adulterous wife but also children conceived in unfaithfulness. The Bible story does not specify which ones were Hosea's and which were results of her waywardness. But evidently he cared for them all as though they were his own.

God even told the prophet what to name the children. And they were strange names! Hosea called the oldest Jezreel, after a bloody massacre in Israel that grieved God's heart. The second, a daughter, he designated Lo-Ruhamah, "not loved," for God was warning Israel that His love for the nation had limits. The day was coming when He would have to turn away His love. The third, another boy, received the name Lo-Ammi, meaning "not my people."

God was saying to Israel, "You who have been My very own special people will no longer be My people, and I will no longer be your God. I cannot put up with your infidelities forever."

But God always held out the promise that repentance and obedience would bring about reinstatement. "Yet the Israelites will be like the sand on the seashore, which cannot be measured or counted. In the place where it was said to them, 'You are not my people,' they will be called 'sons of the living God'" (Hosea 1:10). "I will show my love to the one I called 'Not my loved one.' I will say to those called 'Not my people,' 'You are my people'; and they will say, 'You are my God'" (Hosea 2:23).

Israel's leaders finally crucified the Son of God when He came to earth, leaving these glorious promises to be fulfilled through spiritual Israel. But what hope the story of Hosea gives us as we see enacted in a human family the lavishness of God's love and forgiveness!

We don't know how many times Hosea had to seek a runaway wife. Chapter 3 tells us of one such incident. God told the prophet to go after his unfaithful wife and bring her back home. He was to keep on loving her even though she sought other lovers, just as God loved the Israelites even though they turned to other gods.

Hosea recounts the pitiful story: "So I bought her for fifteen shekels of silver and about a homer and a lethek [about 10 bushels] of barley. Then I told her, 'You are to live with me many days; you must not be a prostitute or be intimate with any man, and I will live with you'" (Hosea 3:2, 3).

Was there a happy ending to the story of Gomer and Hosea? I'd like to think that she was finally able to accept his love, that she lost her fear and restlessness, and that she fell in love with Hosea and became the faithful mother of her children. The Bible doesn't tell us the ending, perhaps because it would take our minds off the important picture of God that the experience portrays.

The story of Hosea and Gomer is still relevant today. God is calling His wife—His church—to turn away from other lovers, to bear children of faithfulness. The Lord calls us into the arms of a loving marriage.

Through the inspiration of the Holy Spirit King Solomon wrote a small but very moving book of the Bible that some people hesitate to read because of the openness of the love and passion expressed between the lover and the beloved. But when you come to understand that God is the lover and we are the beloved, the book has great meaning.

God is open in His love and passion for us. Listen to how the lover speaks of the beauty of the beloved:

"How beautiful you are, my darling!
Oh, how beautiful! . . .
All beautiful you are, my darling;
    there is no flaw in you. . . .
You have stolen my heart, my sister, my bride;

> you have stolen my heart
> with one glance of your eyes."
>
> —Song of Solomon 4:1-9

And let's eavesdrop as the ideal beloved confides to her friends about the relationship between her lover and herself: "He has taken me to the banquet hall, and his banner over me is love" (S. of Sol. 2:4). The *Clear Word* renders it as "He invited me to a banquet at the palace and told everyone there that he loved me."

That's the way God is—He delights to tell everyone of His love for His bride.

Not only is He open with us, but He longs for us to openly express our love and admiration for Him. The beloved also is willing to make a total commitment to her lover:

> "Place me like a seal over your heart,
> like a seal on your arm;
> for love is as strong as death,
> its jealousy unyielding as the grave.
> It burns like blazing fire,
> like a mighty flame."
>
> —Song of Solomon 8:6

I'll admit that in quoting from the Song of Songs I have been very selective. I began to appreciate this book only when I realized that it was written for a people nomadic in lifestyle who lived close to the soil, close to their animals. Many would not consider many of the descriptive phrases in the Song of Songs as appropriate today. Few women I know would consider being compared to a flock of goats or sheep as acceptable love language. But in Solomon's day this was high praise. What we should examine in this book is the passion, the strength of the love relationship that God wants to have with His bride, His wife, His church. He will share her with no one else.

When God spoke the Ten Commandments from Mount Sinai, He clearly stated the kind of association He wanted with His people—one-on-one, with no one else intruding. "I am the only true God, the God who led you out of Egypt. You are to worship Me and no other," God told the people. "Don't make any idols as the heathen do, and worship them. I am a jealous God. I won't share your heart" (paraphrase of Ex. 20:1-5).

Throughout Hebrew history we find that God's greatest complaint against His people was that they were untrue to Him, seeking other lovers. God's jealousy is a holy passion for the pure love of His bride.

He wants to hear us say to each other:

"Come, let us return to the Lord.
He has torn us to pieces
but he will heal us;
he has injured us
but he will bind up our wounds."

—Hosea 6:1

---

\* *Achor* means "trouble."

## CHAPTER 6

### *Captivated by the Beauty of the Bride*

Our Thanksgiving and Christmas holidays that year were only an anticlimax to the big fall event of our family, the first grandchild's wedding. Melissa, at 19, was much too young (according to her grandmother) to be a bride. But she had already finished two years of college, spent several months in the reality of the work world, and declared that she had found the perfect mate. Even her parents had to admit that David fit into the family amazingly well.

And so my husband agreed to perform the ceremony and tie the knot. It was a double blessing for my husband that weekend. Melissa's youngest brother was ready for baptism, and it was planned that Grandpa would baptize Timmy on Sabbath and marry Melissa and David on Sunday. All on one trip. Very well planned.

Melissa was a lovely bride, fresh in the beauty of her youth. David was the happiest looking bridegroom I have ever seen. His whole face glowed as he watched Melissa walk down the aisle toward him on the arm of her father, our youngest son, Tom. The entire family was involved. Little sister Aarika, nearly 3, was the flower girl. Brothers Tommy and Timmy served as groomsmen and ushers. Judy, Melissa's amazing mother, who coordinated the event, was almost as lovely as the bride, even after planning and executing a fantastic wedding for her eldest.

The whole family gathered around to celebrate: Great-aunt Wanda and Great-uncle Chuck from Oklahoma; Great-grandma, aged 97, from her nearby guest home; Great-aunt Christine and Great-uncle Al; Great-aunt Ruth Ann from Tennessee; Great-uncle Clayton from Kentucky; Aunt Lori; Aunt Mary; Uncle John; numerous cousins—and two sets of grandparents, plus all the groom's family and the hundreds of guests. It was a fairyland wedding.

But I'm thinking of another bride, another wedding, another happy Groom entirely captivated by the beauty of His bride. The wedding is soon to take place. And the bride is preparing for the occasion when her Groom will come to take her to the home He has prepared.

What does Scripture tell us about God, the Bridegroom, and the church, His bride?

Several times throughout my husband's and my church ministry I have received invitations to speak at a wedding or an anniversary reception in honor of marriage. The first time I very confidently turned to the Bible, expecting to find an example of a perfect marriage to use as an illustration. I researched thoroughly the best-known Bible couples I could find described in Scripture. But my conclusions disturbed me:

Couple number 1: Adam and Eve were the best-known married couple of all time. God Himself performed their marriage ceremony under ideal circumstances. Yet they began having problems while they were still on their honeymoon.

Couple number 2: Abraham and Sarah were willing to leave the rest of their family and follow God into the unknown. Yet they had serious problems with another woman in their marriage.

Couple number 3: Isaac and Rebekah caused friction in

their relationship as soon as their twin sons were born by each parent choosing a favorite son.

Couple number 4: Jacob and Rachel fell in love at first sight. Yet they seemed to have everything against them from the very beginning. There were always more than two in their marriage.

Couple number 5: David and Bathsheba founded their marriage upon adultery and murder.

Couple number 6: Hosea, a young prophet, courted and married a prostitute, Gomer. Their marriage progressed much as we might have guessed it would with that beginning, Hosea patiently forgiving Gomer's infidelities and time after time taking her back and parenting the children of her adultery.

Please don't accuse me of picking out poor examples—these are the best the Bible has to offer! Why? Why didn't God give us an impressive list of perfect marriages for us to pattern after? Why are the couples I've listed the most outstanding of the Bible in spite of their problems? How are we, the people of God, to know how to behave as Christ's bride if we have no good examples?

As I contemplated this dilemma it crossed my mind that we need to learn to think differently. The Bible makes it plain that God looks at people and situations in a wholly different way than we do. For example, He saw David—the same David who committed adultery and murder—as perfect! The king was perfect in God's sight because of his deep repentance and faith, not because he did everything right. Throughout the Bible we find ourselves astounded at its almost brutal frankness and lack of cover-up. Scripture never hides anyone's faults. From its stories we learn much about the human heart and human relationships. We discover that no human relationship is to be our guide. Bible illustrations often contrast with the ideal rather than give us a model to follow.

But God did give us a perfect example to pattern marriage after. Not through a perfect human couple, but through a symbol. God's symbol of marriage throughout both the Old and New Testaments is His relationship with His church: the husband, God, and His wife, the people He chose to be His very own, just as every husband selects a wife.

But even this symbol gives us a less than ideal picture despite God's perfection, because of the waywardness of His bride—His chosen people, you and me. We've already seen this in the story of Hosea and Gomer.

Yet the Bible enlarges this symbol so that we may use it for a pattern. Jesus Christ came and lived as a human being— *took our place*—so *He* became a symbol of the bride just as He was the representative of the chosen people. His perfect relationship with God, the Supreme Ruler, the Father, and the Husband, is the model for all our relationships.

So you see, we should never shape our marriages here on earth after human ones. Our only measurement is Christ, our example. God gives us no record of a human marriage without problems or of people without faults. What the Bible does is to list many good marriages and tell of the problems the couples met and overcame, thus giving us hope for victory ourselves.

God loves us no less because of our faults.

"I have loved you," God said through Jeremiah, "with an everlasting love; I have drawn you with loving-kindness" (Jer. 31:3).

Since I wrote the first draft of this chapter another granddaughter has married. Another glorious, exciting weekend as another happy bride and groom began a new home—another blissful happy groom! Again I thought of

God's joy as He finally brings His bride home.

If we could only learn to love as God does! In my research on marriages I came across a verse by Sara Teasdale, well-known American poet, that expresses the kind of love a husband and wife must have for each other in order to be truly one:

> "They came to tell your faults to me,
> They named them over one by one;
> I laughed aloud when they were done,
> I knew them all so well before—
> Oh, they were blind, too blind to see
> Your faults had made me love you more."

In Hosea we see that God states His plan to "allure" His bride, to speak "tenderly" to her, and to open before her "a door of hope." That door of hope helps us to view a picture of God that we have never witnessed before. And to see others through His eyes!

With that in mind, looking through God's eyes, let's take a look at His captivating bride and her relationship with her Lover. Let's watch her wedding preparations and even catch a glimpse of the honeymoon plans!

God can see the end from the beginning. He knows the outcome of earth's whole sad history. I'm so glad He included the book of Revelation in the Bible so that we could catch a bit of His excitement at the end of the story. For if God's Word is true, someday soon God's bride will be ready for the wedding. Yes, her lovely linen wedding gown will be perfectly fashioned, all her questions and doubts satisfied, and her face will reveal perfect trust in her perfect Husband.

> " 'Hallelujah!
> For our Lord God Almighty reigns.
> Let us rejoice and be glad

and give him glory!
For the wedding of the Lamb has come,
and his bride has made herself ready.
Fine linen, bright and clean,
was given her to wear.'
(Fine linen stands for the righteous acts of the saints.)

Then the angel said to me, 'Write: Blessed are those who are invited to the wedding supper of the Lamb!' And He added, 'These are the true words of God' " (Rev. 19:6-9).

We don't have to understand perfectly how this can be—but we must individually have hearts responding to the love of our Bridegroom, our Redeemer. God's love will change us into His image. Remember that He does not perceive us as we might view one another or even as we see ourselves. He looks on the heart.

The wilderness sanctuary outlines the relationship that the church must have with God in order to be prepared for His second coming: obedience to the Ten Commandments, a growing understanding of the righteousness of Christ, an intimate daily personal relationship with God, and mercy and love toward one another.

In the final book of the Bible God gives us an overview of earth's history through specific messages to seven actual churches active at the time when the apostle John received the vision, yet also prophetic of seven consecutive historical periods of time, concluding at the end of the world. In the vision God shows His church, the bride of Christ, throughout the lifetime of the world. The seventh and last church is called Laodicea.

In His counsel to the church in Laodicea Jesus tells us that His bride is not yet ready for the wedding. Although she thinks she has everything she needs, the dress she is trying to make for herself will never do for such a royal celebration. As Jesus looks down from heaven upon the one He loves, He sees her as "pitiful, poor, blind, and naked!" What a sad commentary from the Bridegroom she loves so much. But He does not give up on His bride.

Jesus says that He can tell her how to get ready. "I counsel you to buy from me gold refined in the fire, so you can become rich; and white clothes to wear, so you can cover your shameful nakedness; and salve to put on your eyes, so you can see" (Rev. 3:18).

Jesus both points out to His bride her terrible unreadiness for the wedding and shows her just what she lacks. Although He asks her to "buy" these things, elsewhere in Scripture we find that when God asks us to buy something, it is without money (Isa. 55:1, 2)! He *gives us* what we need in exchange for our whole heart. So, to paraphrase, Jesus is saying here, "Give Me your whole heart, and you will become rich in faith and love. Accept My free gift of a beautiful white wedding dress composed of My own righteousness. When you are ready, I will come back for you as My bride."

He continues, "To him [My bride] who overcomes, I will give the right to sit with me on my throne, just as I overcame and sat down with my Father on his throne" (Rev. 3:21).

A day will come when all the preparations will be finished and the wedding will take place. My pastor husband tells me that for him the most thrilling part of each wedding that he performs is when he asks the bride and groom to face each other and say their vows. Just imagine Christ and His bride, the church, gazing at each other, holding hands.

The Father asks, "Do You, Jesus, take this woman to be Your wife forever? Will You cherish her, care for her throughout all eternity?"

Jesus' face beams at His bride. "Oh, yes," He pledges, "I will."

The Father turns to the beautiful white-clothed bride. "Do you take this Man to be your husband forever? Will you cherish Him, honor Him, obey Him throughout all eternity?"

With one voice the redeemed bride, the church, at last face-to-face with Jesus, responds, "I will. Forever and ever I am Your wife, and You are my Husband."

The honeymoon plans? Not a two-week honeymoon— or even a month. No, Jesus plans 1,000 years of exploring the beauties of the universe with His bride!

John the revelator describes the scene at the close of the honeymoon. He sees the New Jerusalem, filled with the redeemed from earth who live there in the homes that Jesus has made for them, as it descends from heaven to earth. The apostle portrays the city as being "prepared as a bride beautifully dressed for her husband" (Rev. 21:2). An angel calls out to John, "Come, I will show you the bride, the wife of the Lamb" (verse 9). At that moment the apostle gets transported to where he can clearly see and identify the composition of that glorious city and the details of its beauty.

God sets the city in place where the Mount of Olives is located, the very place the disciples stood as they watched Jesus ascend into heaven after His resurrection. As the redeemed look upon the devastation of the earth the mighty voice of Jesus calls the wicked from their graves, and they gather together with Satan and his evil angels. The throng of wicked humanity, led by Satan and his demons, surround the Holy City as if to take it by storm. Events follow in quick succession. A glorious throne appears high over the city, and a giant screen begins to portray the lives of all those gathered outside the city. Heaven pronounces final judgment and passes out the sentences. For the first time the wicked find themselves face to face with God. All in that great crowd bow to acknowledge the greatness and majesty of the

Almighty. They realize that He has given them every opportunity possible for salvation, and they confess that His love, mercy, and justice are boundless. Yet their wicked hearts remain unchanged. Unable to endure the brightness of God's face, they are consumed by the fire of His presence.

Inside the city God's bride—the host of the redeemed—shed their last tears of sorrow for the lost as they watch the flames consume the entire surface of the earth. The fire destroys all traces of sin. Satan and his demons can no longer tempt humanity to sin. Sin is no more. God has wiped away all tears. The entire universe is harmonious forever.

The Holy Three re-create the earth in Edenic beauty. Jesus and His bride have come to their eternal home. At long last the earth will fulfill the purpose for which God created it.

## The Face of God

### in

### "I Am Your Husband and You Are My Wife"

Since Eden, when God introduced Adam to Eve, marriage has been a part of God's plan for humanity. God describes the tie of love and desire for each other that a husband and wife share as becoming "one flesh" when they speak their marriage vows. When God declares that He is our Husband and we are His wife, He shows us the depth of the union He plans to have with us.

In the story of Hosea and Gomer the Lord illustrated before humanity the unconditional love that He has for His church, the depth of His forgiveness, and the strategies to which He will go to woo her for His own. We see the face of God as a Husband, tender and loving but also passionate and jealous, unwilling to share her with other lovers.

In the New Testament we see the Son of God, Jesus, as the Husband, and His followers as the bride that He has chosen for His very own. Although faulty and frail, the bride is beautiful in the eyes of her divine Lover. He has set His heart on being able to live with her throughout eternity.

God sees her faults—but offers remedy for them.

"Buy of Me the gold of faith and love," He counsels, "and salve for your eyes so that you can truly see, and accept the white wedding dress I have prepared for you, My beloved, out of My own righteousness" (paraphrase of Revelation 3:18).

God longs with passionate desire for the great wedding day when He can take His bride home.

## PART IV

## *"I Am the Potter and You Are the Clay"*

This is the word that came to Jeremiah
from the Lord:
'Go down to the potter's house,
and there I will give you my message.'
So I went down to the potter's house,
and I saw him working at the wheel.
But the pot he was shaping from the clay
was marred in his hands;
so the potter formed it into another pot,
shaping it as seemed best to him.
Then the word of the Lord came to me:
'O house of Israel,
can I not do with you as this potter does?'
declares the Lord.
'Like clay in the hand of the potter,
so are you in my hand, O house of Israel.' "
—Jeremiah 18:1-6

"O Lord, you are our Father.
We are the clay, you are the potter;
we are all the work of your hand."
—Isaiah 64:8

CHAPTER 7

## *In the Hands of the Potter*

Cooking pots, waterpots, dishes, vases—all were fashioned by skilled artisans from clay during Bible times. People in many areas constructed their homes of clay bricks. Scribes wrote records on clay tablets. How interesting that God sent the prophet Jeremiah to watch the process of forming earthenware in order to illustrate His personal relationship with His special people.

It happened first in heaven—created beings deciding that they were as important, as powerful, as God the Creator Himself. Lucifer challenged Him for the position of ruler of the universe—a role he was totally unable to fill. His inflated ego wouldn't let him realize that he was nothing until touched by the Creator's power.

How did God respond to the challenge? He spoke a world into existence in the presence of the entire universe. Then He formed human beings out of its dust. They were nothing but clay forms until God breathed into them the breath of life.

The watching universe could clearly see that the relationship between the Creator and the created was never between two equals, but always between One who was eternal, all-powerful and all-wise, and the creatures He created in His image. God longed for intelligent beings who would respond to His love—who would walk and talk with Him—yet who would worship Him as their Creator and humble themselves to His leading.

But the dreadful miasma of sin quickly reached the perfect new world. The man and woman God had created to be His companions fell prey to Lucifer's temptation, and the darkness of sin separated them from the Godhead. Sadly enough, the majority of their descendants, as had Lucifer, coveted the power of the Most High. They ignored the implications of the potter and the clay.

Through the prophet Isaiah God challenged them:

"You turn things upside down,

as if the potter were thought to be like the clay!

Shall what is formed say to him who formed it,

'He did not make me'?

Can the pot say of the potter,

'He knows nothing'?"

—Isaiah 29:16

Boundaries surround and protect the relationship that God desires to have with humanity. Although it takes at least two to make any covenant or agreement, they need not be equal. Consider the electric company and its agreement to furnish us with energy for our homes. It's obvious that the electric company has all the power, while we have all the need. As human beings we often make deals with the strong to supplement our lack. When we make an agreement with God, the inequality is to our eternal advantage.

Because joined to our weakness is His strength, His abundance to our poverty, His light to our darkness, His life to our death.

We are the blessed ones when we accept this agreement signed by the blood of Jesus!

Ellen White comments: "The potter takes the clay and

88

molds it according to his will. He kneads it and works it. He tears it apart and presses it together. He wets it and then dries it. He lets it lie for a while without touching it. When it is perfectly pliable, he continues the work of making of it a vessel. He forms it into shape and on the wheel trims and polishes it. He dries it in the sun and bakes it in the oven. Thus it becomes a vessel fit for use. So the great Master Worker desires to mold and fashion us. And as the clay is in the hands of the potter, so are we to be in His hands. We are not to try to do the work of the potter. Our part is to yield ourselves to be molded by the Master Worker."*

The Bible writers add still another metaphor to describe God's work in molding and perfecting human beings—that of refining silver:

> "Therefore this is what the Lord Almighty says:
> 'See, I will refine and test them,
> for what else can I do
> because of the sin of my people?' "
> —Jeremiah 9:7

"But who can endure the day of his coming? Who can stand when he appears? For he will be like a refiner's fire or a launderer's soap. He will sit as a refiner and purifier of silver; he will purify the Levites and refine them like gold and silver. Then the Lord will have men [and women] who will bring offerings in righteousness" (Mal. 3:2, 3).

I like the story of a present-day man whose work involved refining silver. When asked how he knew when the process was complete, he responded, "When I can see the reflection of my face in it."

When God can see the reflection of His character in us, He will know that we are ready to take home.

Often the natural human response to the process of refining is to feel that it is harming us. We may even demand,

"Why are You doing this to me, God?" Yet it is the only way that we can grow in the Lord.

> "See, I have refined you, though not as silver;
>> I have tested you in the furnace of affliction."
>>> —Isaiah 48:10

> "This third I will bring into the fire;
>> I will refine them like silver
>> and test them like gold.
> They will call on my name
>> and I will answer them;
> I will say, 'They are my people,'
> and they will say, 'The Lord is our God.'"
>> —Zechariah 13:9

Notice the response of the people being refined in the previous passage. They call on the Lord—pray—and God assures them, "You are My people." Their joyful response is "The Lord is our God." They recognize God's hand in their affliction.

"O people of Zion, who live in Jerusalem, you will weep no more. How gracious he will be when you cry for help! As soon as he hears, he will answer you. Although the Lord gives you the bread of *adversity* and the water of *affliction, your teachers* will be hidden no more; with your own eyes you will see them. Whether you turn to the right or to the left, your ears will hear a voice behind you, saying, 'This is the way; walk in it'" (Isa. 30:19-21).

I came across this passage in Isaiah when I was in the midst of the greatest trial of my life—an estrangement from a beloved family member. It seemed to me that my worst nightmare had come true. Gone were my fluent prayers—I had been unable to pray anything except "Help!" for days. And to top that off, I felt that God had turned His face away from me, that heaven's door had closed just when I needed Him the most. I was in agony.

Through Isaiah the Holy Spirit whispered that God heard my heart-cry. And not only had He heard it, but He was answering me! At the time I wasn't sure I liked His answers as He took His potter's tool to my wounded soul.

Yet as I look back on those days I praise God for allowing me to come to my "wits' end," as David says of the people in Psalm 107:27. I had to face up to the fact that my premise that a mother could work out any family problem if she loved enough and tried hard enough simply was not true. All humanity is helpless in the face of many events. I could not change them or make them better. All I could do was pray.

Although I have yet seen no miraculous healing in the estranged family relationship that I faced that day, I have learned to leave this battle with God. The most amazing result was that God immediately gave me a ministry for Him! Sure that I was useless since I could not heal the damage in my own family, I wondered how I could be a blessing to anyone else. Yet God opened to me a ministry to other hurting souls in ways beyond my wildest imagination. I still don't understand it.

Not for a moment do I believe that God caused the adversity in my life, but He surely used it as a powerful tool to lead me to realize that I needed a deeper relationship with Him than I had ever had before.

Adversity and affliction are often the teachers that God sends His faithful followers so that they will learn to recognize His voice in their lives. When His hand is the potter's hand, His stroke is sure and swift and brings healing to the soul. He can then mold us into something beautiful and useful for His kingdom.

Remember the old song?

> "Have Thine own way, Lord! Have Thine own way!
> Thou art the Potter; I am the clay.
> Mold me and make me after Thy will,
> While I am waiting, yielded and still."

---

* Ellen G. White, *The Ministry of Healing* (Mountain View, Calif.: Pacific Press Pub. Assn., 1905), pp. 471, 472.

CHAPTER 8

## *Perfect Design*

Before my birth God had a plan for my life:
> "For you created my inmost being;
>> you knit me together in my mother's womb.
> I praise you because I am fearfully and wonder-
>> fully made;
>> Your works are wonderful,
>> I know that full well.
> My frame was not hidden from you
>> when I was made in the secret place.
> When I was woven together in the depths of the
>> earth,
>> your eyes saw my unformed body.
> All the days ordained for me
>> were written in your book
>> before one of them came to be."
> —Psalm 139:13-16

God knew my mother and father, the place I was born, the situation of my upbringing. He knew my IQ, my personality, and the genetics of my body. The Lord knew my inheritance and my environment. And, in spite of the imperfections of my beginnings, He had a perfect design for my life.

"For we are God's workmanship, created in Christ Jesus

to do good works, which God *prepared in advance for us to do"* (Eph. 2:10).

Scripture clearly tells us that God devised a plan so that each of us can be saved. "But we ought always to thank God for you, brothers loved by the Lord, because *from the beginning God chose you to be saved* through the sanctifying work of the Spirit and through belief in the truth" (2 Thess. 2:13).

What a joy it is to realize that God's plan involves making us into the likeness of His Son, Jesus!

"And we know that in all things God works for the good of those who love him, *who have been called according to his purpose.* For those God foreknew *He also predestined to be conformed to the likeness of his Son,* that he might be the firstborn among many brothers" (Rom. 8:28, 29).

Beforehand God recorded in heaven my day-by-day development and the final finished product (Ps. 139:16). He had a perfect character designed for me.

Of course, the problem is that I botched it! Yes, I spoiled His perfect plan.

How does God handle this? Well, to begin with, He knew this would occur. It happens with all of us. But even this horrid blotch God works into His perfect plan. Of course, I can thwart the forwarding of His design by my rebelliousness, but it is still available at any time I choose to cooperate with Him. I may waste the best years of my life in my waywardness, as did King Solomon, and have only regret in my old age. But God can, with my cooperation, still re-create in me His perfect goal. This is the glory of redemption. Like the potter, God can take broken things and make them over anew. God says: "I will repay you for the years the locusts [of sin] have eaten" (Joel 2:25).

I am not saying that a wasted life has no consequences. What we might have done had we consistently cooperated with God's plan, but did not accomplish through our neglect or rebelliousness, will produce an eternal loss.[1] All of us will have this to reckon with, some more than others.

But God has given us examples of how He can accomplish His preplanned design even though people have devastated most of their lives. King Manasseh, son of Hezekiah, was the epitome of wickedness, leading the people of Judah into sins more evil than those of the pagan nations around them. When God spoke to him, he refused to listen. Finally the Lord allowed the Assyrian army to take Manasseh captive, leading him away with a hook in his nose!

The situation got the king's attention. "In his distress he sought the favor of the Lord his God and humbled himself greatly before the God of his fathers. And when he prayed to him, the Lord was moved by his entreaty and listened to his plea; so he brought him back to Jerusalem and to his kingdom. Then Manasseh knew that the Lord is God" (2 Chron. 33:12, 13).

The Bible relates that the reinstated ruler destroyed the false gods in his kingdom and their cult sites and restored the worship of the true deity. God was able to complete in Manasseh His perfect design.

The apostle Paul is another example of restoration after a life of rebellion. The memory of his past persecutions of Christians haunted him the rest of his life.

We human beings are so performance-oriented that it is hard for us to see how it is that God can take even a sordid past and work it into a perfect design. He does not keep remembering the past. He forgives and washes it away. Yet the lessons we learn from our experiences in sin He can use in our character-building. Our weaknesses teach us never to trust ourselves again, to loathe sin and avoid it at all cost.

God begins by retraining our minds: "Therefore, I urge

you, brothers, in view of God's mercy, to offer your bodies as living sacrifices, holy and pleasing to God—this is your spiritual act of worship. Do not conform any longer to the pattern of this world, but be transformed by the *renewing of your mind.* Then you will be able to *test and approve what God's will is—his good, pleasing and perfect will"* (Rom. 12:1, 2).

Our retrained mind's automatic response to temptation will be to test it by God's Word. "It is written" will be our guideline. So as we cooperate with Him in our transformation we must learn to obey His laws not just from the *emotion* of love, but from the *principle* of love.

Many of us are impulsive in our spiritual life. Some days we feel very spiritual, less so other days. One of my recent prayers to the Lord has been that He would make me "strong, firm, and steadfast" so that I will never waver in His service, no matter what my fleeting emotions of the day seem to be. The promise is: "And the God of all grace, who called you to his eternal glory in Christ, after you have suffered a little while, will himself restore you and make you *strong, firm and steadfast.* To him be the power for ever and ever. Amen" (1 Peter 5:10, 11).

This verse tells us that suffering must be the prelude to strength and steadiness. The promise of eventual restoration to God's perfect plan for my character makes it bearable. But in order for suffering to be effective in working restoration, I must *learn* from it.

Satan has a clever little tactic that he has practiced since sin entered our world. If he can bypass the control center of the mind and plug directly into the unconscious mind, we impulsively respond in any situation by repeating what we have always done in the past or by reacting with our emotions alone, thus learning nothing. God desires to teach us His principles and to firmly implant them in the control center of our minds so that our characters can grow.

Much as we dislike pain, it often seems that the best way we learn is through it. When I realize that God is the faithful Potter who is willing to take the time to shape and reshape this lump of clay into the perfect plan He has for my life—not only here on earth but for eternity—I am humbled. But how is God ever going to accomplish this? History seems to repeat itself endlessly. How are we ever going to learn? Let's answer that question by reviewing the story of this book thus far.

All heaven is involved in humanity's salvation. The spellbinding story unfolding on our small dark planet absorbs the attention of the entire universe. First we examined the picture of the Almighty declaring to the descendants of one family, "I will be your God, and you will be My people." Then we focused on Jesus, Son of God, Son of man—His pivotal role in the struggle on earth as He identified Himself with human beings. But the Godhead includes another personality—the Holy Spirit. The special role of the Holy Spirit is to prepare a people to display God's glory on earth. It is His special mission to develop in each of us that intimate relationship with God that will make the future different from the past.

The Bible stories I've recounted in the first two chapters—God's choosing a special people to be His very own, and God's own words of love and yearning for His people—have warmed my heart and thrilled my soul. But I find a different reaction among the people who actually lived out those stories.

For instance, God performed amazing miracles for the people He had chosen to be His own. Although they were slaves in Egypt—the greatest nation in the then-known world—God led them to freedom in great style, climaxed by allowing them to march through the Red Sea on dry land while the returning waves swallowed up the enemies who pursued them. No god of the Egyptians had ever given such a demonstration. The former slaves rejoiced at their freedom. But when God spoke in an audible voice from the top of a burning mountain, giving laws for them to live by, how did the people respond? Were they grateful? Did they sense His love and His intimate presence?

No, they didn't seem to. His mighty power and the fearsome acts He performed seemed only to frighten them. "When the people saw the thunder and lightning and heard the trumpet and saw the mountain in smoke, they trembled with fear. They stayed at a distance and said to Moses, 'Speak to us yourself and we will listen. But do not have God speak to us or we will die'" (Ex. 20:18, 19).

Throughout the biblical accounts of the Israelite nation we find similar passages. The majority of the people always seemed to stay at a distance from God. His mighty acts in behalf of His people did not seem to lead to the love relationship He desired to have with His people.

The Jewish nation recounted the thrilling stories of those early days again and again. Odes to the great God who performed mighty miracles for them, in contrast to the helpless gods of the nations around them, fill Jewish literature. But did it draw the people into intimacy with Him? The answer seems to be "Very rarely." Fear is a deterrent to friendship. And since they lacked that total friendship with the Creator-God, God's chosen people often worshiped pagan deities with whom they seemed to feel more comfortable.

Was the fault with God? Did He choose poor methods to draw the people to Him? Of course not. God always knows what is best. But because of His perfect character of love there are certain guidelines by which He always works:

He never varies from *truth;*
He always respects our *freedom;*
He is not limited by *time;*
He uses no force other than *love.*[2]

Yes, God grieved at their fear. But He understood that until they realized His mighty power and knew Him as a creative God, they could never really grasp Him at all. He left them free to hold Him at a distance—or to come close. And some—like Moses—approached Him in spite of their initial fear. Enoch, Abraham, Moses, Job, David—individuals such as these were all counted as God's friends.

Down through the generations some of the fear seeped away. Reading about or hearing about an incident is less fearful than experiencing it. Yet God often holds His power in check when He longs to step in and do more for His people. He stands back only to give us room for comfort.

Throughout Scripture and history we see God at work wooing His people, drawing them to Himself, seeking to develop an intimate love relationship with them that will lead them to trust Him fully.

What about His people today? Will the God of the last generation on earth have to hold Himself back to keep His people comfortable? Or will He have a people who know Him so well that He is free to repeat the mighty acts of the past—and even excel them? Will those He has called to be His special people hide in the rocks in fear at His coming—or will they shout, "This is our God! We have waited for Him"?

As we look to the past we see failure. God's people never lived up to the potential He had for them. When Jesus—God Himself—came to reveal the divine character to the children of Israel, their leaders killed Him. Finally He turned away from them sadly and began a new people.

Will we be any different than the children of Israel? Will we prove faithful, or will God have to give up on us, too? What has to happen to make the people of God a glory to His name?

When God created human beings, He made us unique and special beings. Not only did He give us life, but He made us in His image. He planned that we would always be included in the circle of His selfless love—we in God, He in us. The Lord provided a special place in our minds that only His presence would satisfy. When Adam and Eve sinned, self took God's place in their hearts. But self always leaves empty corners in the special spot He designed for the Holy Spirit. We always have a longing for something more. The Lord created humans with the desire to worship Him, and the emptiness of their fallen self-centered spirit leads them to create their own gods. Thus we see idolatry, lust, love of money, desire for power, and the numerous gods of our time.

The solution? Something He designed in heaven before He created the earth.

And what is that plan?

He revealed it when He asked Moses to build the sanctuary in the wilderness. As I studied the daily, weekly, and yearly work of the priests, I caught a glimpse of what God desired of me and what He had made provision for me to have in intimacy with the entire Godhead. This changed my life.

I saw that the lamps in the tabernacle, faithfully tended by the priests so that the light always continued to burn, symbolized God's plan for each of us individually. Daily trimming is necessary in our lives to keep the light of the Holy Spirit glowing in our hearts. The hand of the Holy Spirit is the gentlest and kindest tool the heavenly potter can use. I suspect that many of the lessons we learn in hard trial and pain we could have acquired more gently had we only kept the lamp of the Holy Spirit trimmed in our daily relationship with Him.

The plan that heaven has for each of us to live fruitful and holy lives in His service involves the entire Godhead. Before They created the world, God the Father, God the Son, and God the Holy Spirit devised a way to enable Jesus to live a holy life after His birth into the human race. We see it working in Jesus during His days on earth. It is vital that we carefully study the life of Jesus and ask God for guidance on how to reflect His example.

The Bible tells us that Jesus was born of the Spirit. From His childhood on, Jesus let the Holy Spirit guide and teach Him. Throughout His adolescence and adulthood Jesus remained in constant communication with His Father through the Spirit. It was the Holy Spirit who led Him into the wilderness after His baptism, daily called Him to prayer, and continually showed Him what to pray for. Before every important decision He spent hours in prayer. He prayed all night before He chose the 12 to be His closest disciples.

God desires to have us walk with Him in the same way. Long before we make the choice to accept Christ as our Savior and Lord, the Holy Spirit woos us, calls us. And after our new birth all the resources of heaven are ours through the Holy Spirit. The apostle Paul describes this daily intimacy with God as keeping step with the Spirit or walking in the Spirit.

The Face of God

in

"I Am the Potter and You Are the Clay"

As we viewed God as a high and holy being in chapter 1 we focused in on the eternal face of God as the Creator and humanity as those He created. Never can that line be blurred—never in all eternity. God will always be deity, and we the work of His hands.

A creature can never become God. Lucifer overlooked that impossibility, and humanity still follows in his footsteps. Through the potter and clay illustration God clearly defines the relationship that He will always have with His people—Creator and created.

God has a perfect plan for our lives, and if we comply— rest secure in the Potter's hands—that plan will be fulfilled. The Lord longs to have a people who trust Him completely and recognize His voice and His work in their lives. It is for this very reason that He shapes and polishes those He loves. Like silver He refines us until He can see His face in us. Not only does God recognize our likeness to Him, but the world will also see His glory in His people.

It is because of God's persistence in His Potter's work that we can be assured that history will not keep on repeating itself, a pattern of sinning and repenting, sinning and repenting, and sinning again. One day the Lord will have a people so molded and polished that He can trust them to remain true to Him throughout eternity. The devil, his angels, sinners, and everything pertaining to sin will be destroyed.

---

[1] See Ellen G. White, *Christ's Object Lessons* (Washington, D.C.: Review and Herald Pub. Assn., 1941), p. 363.

[2] I learned these four principles from a talk by Dick Winn.

PART V

### *"I Am the Good Shepherd and You Are My Sheep"*

I am the good shepherd;
I know my sheep and my sheep know me—
just as the Father knows me and I know the Father—
and I lay down my life for the sheep.
I have other sheep that are not of this sheep pen.
I must bring them also.
They too will listen to my voice,
and there shall be one flock and one shepherd."
—John 10:14-16

"For this is what the Sovereign Lord says:
I myself will search for my sheep and look after them.
As a shepherd looks after his scattered flock
when he is with them,
so will I look after my sheep.
I will rescue them from all the places
where they were scattered on a day of clouds and darkness. . . .
You my sheep, the sheep of my pasture, are people,
and I am your God, declares the Sovereign Lord."
—Ezekiel 34:11-31

CHAPTER 9

## *The Heart of a Shepherd*

References to sheep fill the Bible. Perhaps you have noticed the many times sheep enter the biblical stories. Consider a sampling of these sheep stories:

Abel offered a firstborn lamb from his flock as an offering to God, while his brother, Cain, brought fruit of the soil.

When Abraham obeyed God's command to offer his son Isaac as a sacrifice, God provided a male sheep in the bushes to take the son's place.

Jacob spent 14 years tending his uncle Laban's sheep to pay the bride price for his two wives.

Moses was herding sheep when he met God at the burning bush.

David was a shepherd before he became the most famous king of Israel.

Job had 7,000 sheep before he lost not only them but everything else he owned, plus his entire family except for his wife. Later God doubled all his possessions (14,000 sheep) and gave him 10 more children.

Jesus was the Lamb of God from the foundation of the world. Every lamb slain in the sacrificial services for hundreds of years represented His death for the sins of the world.

And so the list goes on. The Word of God gives more prominence to sheep than to any other animal. There must be something that God wants us to learn from sheep. In Bible times raising sheep was a common occupation. Sheep furnished mutton for food and wool for clothing. But sheep also required constant care. Of all farm animals sheep are most likely to be timid and helpless. The job of a shepherd demands carefulness in details and constant watchfulness. They must provide sheep with nourishing grass, fresh water, and a safe place to rest and sleep.

Considering the above requirements for tending sheep, we begin to see why God chose shepherding as a preparation for positions of importance in the kingdom of God. It took a conscientious person to be a good shepherd. Although thoughtless and selfish individuals sometimes got hired to care for sheep, yet under their care the sheep did not flourish. Sheep have many enemies: wolves, bears, lions, and, perhaps the worst of all, humanity itself. True shepherds have to live and eat and sleep with the sheep—they have to actually *love* them.

Biblical shepherds do not drive the sheep—rather, they lead them, carefully picking out the best path for them to travel, the proper grazing ground, the freshest water. The shepherds meet every obstacle before the sheep do.

God used shepherding to purify the characters of some of His greatest representatives:

Jacob—who became the father of a great nation.

Moses—who spent 40 years in the wilderness looking after sheep before he became one of the greatest of all prophets.

David—Israel's king who was also the patriarch in the lineage of Jesus.

Amos—a shepherd of Tekoa who became a prophet and author of one of the books of the Holy Scriptures.

The angels chose a group of shepherds in the hills of

Judea to be the first to know the good news of the birth of the long-awaited Redeemer.

Perhaps it would be worthwhile to become a shepherd!

While most of us know that Scripture points to Bethlehem, the city of David, as the birthplace of Jesus, yet perhaps it isn't as well known that the same prophet who prophesied where He would be born also told of His work as a shepherd. Long before Jesus spoke the comforting words "I am the good Shepherd," Micah had prophesied about Him:

> "He will stand and shepherd his flock
>   in the strength of the Lord,
>   in the majesty of the name of the Lord his God.
>   And they will live securely, for then his greatness
>   will reach to the ends of the earth.
>   And he will be their peace."
>
> —Micah 5:4, 5

Isaiah prophesied of Him:

> "He tends his flock like a shepherd:
>   He gathers the lambs in his arms
>   and carries them close to his heart;
>   he gently leads those that have young."
>
> —Isaiah 40:11

How sad that the learned Jewish teachers who diligently studied the writings of the prophets did not remember such passages and thus recognize the divinity of Jesus when they heard Him speak the blessed words "I am the good shepherd."

Jesus proclaimed these words to the people soon after He healed the eyes of a man born blind. The Pharisees had immediately begun denying that Jesus had healed him despite the obvious fact that the man could now see. The Pharisees were not willing to acknowledge that Jesus might be divine.

Sadly Jesus commented that He had come so that the blind might see and those who could see would become blind.[1]

The Pharisees bristled, recognizing that He was speaking figuratively. "What? Are you intimating that we are blind?"

Jesus then began one of His best-known parables.

"There's only one right way to enter a sheepfold," Jesus told the people, "and that is through the door. I am the door to the sheepfold. Anyone who enters any other way than through Me is a thief or a robber. The shepherd always enters by the door, and the sheep recognize their master's voice and are willing to follow. A shepherd calls each sheep by name."

"Not only am I the door to the sheepfold, but I am also the shepherd," He went on to say. "Good shepherds are willing to lay down their lives for their sheep. Hired people will likely abandon the sheep when danger threatens—but not the true shepherds."

Jesus referred to the dangers that constantly threaten the sheep. The robbers and thieves He has already mentioned—but now He speaks of wild animals such as the wolf. Hired individuals may flee from a wolf, but true shepherds will protect the sheep even to the point of giving their lives for the flock.

"I know My sheep," Jesus states, "just as well as I know My Father and My Father knows Me. My sheep recognize My voice, and they follow Me."

An inspired comment about why true Christians follow Jesus deepens our picture of God as the shepherd:

"It is not the fear of punishment, or the hope of everlasting reward, that leads the disciples of Christ to follow Him. They behold the Saviour's matchless love, revealed throughout His pilgrimage on earth, from the manger of Bethlehem to Calvary's cross, and the sight of Him attracts, it softens and subdues the soul. Love awakens in the heart of the beholders. They hear His voice, and they follow Him." [2]

Jesus surprised the religious leaders—even the disciples—by saying, "I have sheep in other sheepfolds, sheep that do not belong to this flock. Yet they all recognize My voice and follow Me. Someday I will gather them all together, and My flock will be one.

"No one can take My life from Me, but I willingly die for My sheep. The Father has given Me the authority and power to die and to rise again.

"Nothing," Jesus promised the listening throng, "can take My sheep out of My hand, and nothing can take them out of My Father's hand. My Father and I are one."

Too bad some of the crowd had ears but could not hear.

Ellen White adds this description of the shepherd:

"As the shepherd leads his flock over the rocky hills, through forest and wild ravines, to grassy nooks by the riverside; as he watches them on the mountains through the lonely night, shielding from robbers, caring tenderly for the sickly and feeble, his life comes to be one with theirs. A strong and tender attachment unites him to the objects of his care. However large the flock, the shepherd knows every sheep. Every one has its name, and responds to the name at the shepherd's call.

"As an earthly shepherd knows his sheep, so does the divine Shepherd know His flock that are scattered throughout the world. . . .

"Jesus knows us individually, and is touched with the feeling of our infirmities. He knows us all by name. He knows the very house in which we live, the name of each occupant." [3]

I imagine that as Jesus told the parable of the good

shepherd He remembered reading in the ancient scrolls about David the young shepherd and his encounters with wild animals and his fierce devotion to his sheep.

Asaph the psalm writer gives us this descriptive passage of how God called David:

"He chose David his servant
>    and took him from the sheep pens;
> from tending the sheep he brought him
>    to be the shepherd of his people Jacob,
>    of Israel his inheritance.
> And David shepherded them with integrity of heart;
>    with skillful hands he led them."
>                                    —Psalm 78:70-72

One of my favorite stories of David as a shepherd records how he went to Saul's camp to see how his older brothers were faring in the army and to bring them supplies from their father. There David saw the Philistine giant Goliath and heard his taunts. Although no one in the Israelite army was brave enough to battle the giant one on one, David was eager to defend the honor of Israel and Israel's God. But he had trouble persuading his brothers, and later King Saul, that he, young as he was, should be considered a contender for the honor of the country. But David won his case with Saul when he recounted his bravery in protecting his sheep.

"David said to Saul, 'Your servant has been keeping his father's sheep. When a lion or a bear came and carried off a sheep from the flock, I went after it, struck it and rescued the sheep from its mouth. When it turned on me, I seized it by its hair, struck it and killed it. Your servant has killed both the lion and the bear; this uncircumcised Philistine will be like one of them, because he has defied the armies of the living God. The Lord who delivered me from the paw of the lion and the paw of the bear will deliver me from the hand of this Philistine.'

"Saul said to David, 'Go, and the Lord be with you'" (1 Sam. 17:34-37).

We are well acquainted with the rest of this story, with how the young shepherd killed the giant and routed the Philistine army. David's bravery resulted from his experience in protecting his sheep and from the relationship with God he had developed throughout his quiet life as a shepherd far from the cities and villages.

So often we wonder why, if God is our shepherd, He allows trouble and sorrow to come to us. We may even feel that He has forsaken us in our troubles. The following quotation comforts my heart as I remember the grief behind me and look ahead to face what the future holds:

"As the shepherd goes before his sheep, himself first encountering the perils of the way, so does Jesus with His people. . . . The way to heaven is consecrated by the Saviour's footprints. The path may be steep and rugged, but Jesus has traveled that way; His feet have pressed down the cruel thorns, to make the pathway easier for us. *Every burden that we are called to bear He Himself has borne.*"[4]

Jesus told yet another sheep story. His love for all humanity especially attracted the common people, even those the Pharisees labeled "sinners." Jews and Gentiles alike crowded around Him. He turned away no one, played no favorites.

"Now the tax collectors and 'sinners' were all gathering around to hear him. But the Pharisees and the teachers of the law muttered, 'This man welcomes sinners and eats with them.'

"Then Jesus told them this parable: 'Suppose one of you has a hundred sheep and loses one of them. Does he not leave the ninety-nine in the open country and go after the lost sheep until he finds it? And when he finds it, he joyfully puts it on his shoulders and goes home. Then he calls his friends and neighbors together and says, "Rejoice with me; I have found my lost sheep." I tell you that in the same way there will be more rejoicing in heaven over one sinner who repents than over ninety-nine righteous persons who do not need to repent'" (Luke 15:1-7).

Jesus shows us in this parable a glimpse of the loving face of God. No matter how many sheep this shepherd had, he cared for each one individually. God is like that too.

God also revealed Himself as a shepherd to the prophet Ezekiel:

"For this is what the Sovereign Lord says: 'I myself will search for my sheep and look after them. As a shepherd looks after his scattered flock when he is with them, so will I look after my sheep. I will rescue them from all the places where they were scattered on a day of clouds and darkness'" (Eze. 34:11, 12).

Ezekiel defines the meaning of his parable as clearly as Jesus did. He quotes God as saying, "You my sheep, the sheep of my pasture, are people, and I am your God, declares the Sovereign Lord" (verse 31).

The prophet Zephaniah tells how our God Himself rejoices over each of those who have chosen Him:

"The Lord your God is with you,
　　he is mighty to save.
He will take great delight in you,
　　he will quiet you with his love,
　　he will rejoice over you with singing."
　　　　　　　　　　—Zephaniah 3:17

We are safe in the arms of our Shepherd.

---

[1] Throughout the story of the good shepherd I am paraphrasing the

words of Jesus.

[2] E. G. White, *The Desire of Ages,* p. 480.

[3] *Ibid.,* p. 479.

[4] *Ibid.,* p. 480. (Italics supplied.)

## CHAPTER 10

## *Story of a Reluctant Sheep*

I grew up on a goat ranch. My sisters and I romped and skipped with the little kids. We learned how babies come into the world from watching the mother goats give birth. And we thrived on goat milk.

When I grew old enough to understand the good connotations the Bible attributes to sheep and its discrimination against goats, it greatly offended me. Woolly lambs were cute, I had to admit, but as far as I was concerned, sheep were stupid and dull!

Our goat friends had *character*—they were exciting to be around. Whoever saw a sheep tumble and slide down a sand dune just for fun? But even our adult goats were fond of just such shenanigans. And the kids were *always* full of spunk and fun. Given the slightest opportunity, they'd head for the sand dunes or to a rock pile to play king of the mountain.

Yet I'll admit that their offenses were many.

Gaylord, our billy goat, loved to sneak up on us from behind and surprise us with a quick butt to the seat of our coveralls, sending us sprawling on the ground.

One day we came home to discover that an adventurous nanny had forced her way through a hole in the fenced-in backyard, pulled down the clothesline, and trampled Mother's freshly washed clothes in the mud.

Another day, while we were in town, a half-grown kid we girls called Ninny (because of her flighty ways) butted open the door into the house and got into Mother's sewing box and ate up half of her precious collection of dress patterns.

I'm not sure that Mother liked goats.

And I'll never forget the day my father decided it was time I learned how to stake a goat out in our yard. The back hillside was fenced, and the goats roamed free on the rocks, in the gullies, and under the trees. But the front hillside down to the road was completely open. And lots of good grass grew there. Daddy decided to get the goats to mow the grass for him to save on feeding costs as well as to make the yard look better. His method was to fasten a 12-foot chain to the goat, take a mallet and a stake, locate a likely spot in the yard, and hammer the stake into the hard ground. The goat would then chomp off the grass within the 24-foot-diameter circle of yard it could reach. This maneuver worked great for an adult man, tall and strong. It was even possible for a sturdy 9-year-old such as my older sister, who had a penchant for caring for livestock. But for me—a small, thin 7-year-old with a timid nature—it was frightening.

Daddy handed me the mallet, the stake, and the chain attached to a very lively adult female goat. Fearfully I started out. The wise old goat immediately recognized that I was a novice at this sort of thing and decided to have some fun. She circled me again and again, pulling the chain tighter and tighter around my skinny little legs. When I shouted for help, a disgusted Daddy came running, unwound me, and pushed me sobbing toward the house.

As far as I remember, my only goat chores from that day onward were to fill the water troughs occasionally and now and then help with feeding. Although both my sisters learned to milk the goats, no one ever suggested that I try it—and I didn't volunteer. I fed the chickens and became a reluctant expert at washing dishes.

One evening for family worship Daddy read the parable of the sheep and the goats. It started out with enough action to immediately catch our interest.

"When the Son of Man comes in his glory, and all the angels with him, he will sit on his throne in heavenly glory. All the nations will be gathered before him, and he will separate the people one from another as a shepherd separates the sheep from the goats. He will put the sheep on his right and the goats on his left" (Matt. 25:31-33).

The three of us girls scarcely wiggled. Here were our goats in the middle of a Bible story! What would happen next?

We sat spellbound as the story continued. To the sheep on His right hand Jesus said, "Come, you who are blessed by my Father; take your inheritance, the kingdom prepared for you since the creation of the world" (verse 34).

But to the goats on His left hand He announced, "Depart from me, you who are cursed, into the eternal fire prepared for the devil and his angels" (verse 41).

Daddy lost our attention immediately. Three little goat girls didn't want to hear any more of that story. Not when someone treated our goats unjustly.

I was almost an adult before I was able to grasp the message of that parable. Only when I was able to compare the habits and disposition of goats and sheep with an unbiased mind was I able to understand what Jesus was saying. He was not disparaging goats or setting aside sheep as sacred. Rather, He was seeking to show us in an unforgettable illustration how every action counts in our final destiny. It's great for a goat to be careless and zany—that's its nature. But when people act like goats, there is no place for them in the kingdom of God. On the other hand, many of the character-istics of a sheep illustrate God's desire for His people.

In using the shepherd and his sheep as a depiction of our relationship with Him, Jesus did not say that sheep were perfect animals. In fact, their very perverseness made the application all the more appropriate. As Isaiah declares:

"We all, like sheep, have gone astray,

each of us has turned to his own way;

and the Lord has laid on him

the iniquity of us all."

—Isaiah 53:6

From the very beginning of sin on earth the death of an innocent lamb symbolized the enormity of the separation from God that sin has caused for the human race. Only the death of God Himself could offer forgiveness and atone-ment for humanity. And only this could restore the rela-tionship that Adam and Eve knew with God in Eden.

Of course, we know that God is eternal and cannot die. But He, in His foreknowledge, devised a plan so that God, by becoming a human being and living a sinless life, could die in our place, thus acting as both sacrifice and priest.

God introduced His eternal plan to Adam and Eve in Eden, though they caught only a faint glimmer of the intri-cacies of the challenges—the pain and the sorrow—yet to be met to eliminate sin from the universe forever. Throughout the centuries He has sought to open the un-derstanding of His plan to humans willing to listen to Him and to be used in furthering His plan. Enoch was one of the first. Later came Noah. Abraham. Isaac. Jacob. Moses. The list of those God was able to walk and talk with in an inti-mate relationship goes on and on. He called this plan His everlasting covenant with humanity.

When God prepared to lead the descendants of

Abraham out from slavery in Egypt to be His special people in a new land, He called them to the ministry of reaching the whole world with the good news of His eternal covenant. God was doing a new thing! He was using a group of people to make an invisible God visible to the world.

We already glanced at the Passover story when we emphasized that we are each God's firstborn. Now I want to tell it again, this time focusing on the significance of the slain lamb.

Moses, God's spokesperson, asked Pharaoh to let the Hebrews leave Egypt, but the Egyptian king was adamant that the large community of slaves should not leave. In order to get Pharaoh to have a change of heart, the Lord sent plagues upon the Egyptians. Stubbornly the monarch became more and more resistant. Finally God threatened Pharaoh's nation with the tenth and most severe plague of all—the death of all its firstborn, both animals and human beings—if the king would not allow His chosen people to leave.

In preparation for His people's exodus, God instructed Moses to count the month in which He delivered the children of Israel from slavery in Egypt as the first month of a whole new Jewish year. He instructed each family among them that on the tenth day of that new month they were to choose a year-old male sheep or male goat from their flock or herd for a very special purpose. They were to kill the lamb or goat at twilight on the fourteenth day of the month, the day God was to deliver His people, and sprinkle some of the animal's blood on the sides and tops of the doorframes of their houses. Then they were to roast and eat the flesh of the lamb or goat while they stood prepared for flight with everything packed and ready to go.

God promised the Hebrews that although the destroying angel would come at midnight to destroy all the firstborn of Egypt, the angel would pass over every Hebrew home that had blood brushed on its doorframe. The children within those houses would be spared.*

It all happened as God had told them. The people of Israel left Egypt in haste as the Egyptians loudly mourned the death of their firstborn children and animals. The Jews would recount the story throughout the centuries and would celebrate a solemn yearly Passover feast.

After Jesus' baptism in the Jordan John the Baptist greeted Him the next day with the words "Look, the Lamb of God, who takes away the sin of the world!" (John 1:29). Jesus Himself was the Passover Lamb, dying on the fourteenth day of the first month of the Jewish year, hundreds of years after the first Passover. Our salvation is sure only when we by faith continually apply the blood of Jesus on the doorpost of our hearts and homes. Our relationship with God depends upon our acceptance of the blood of Jesus to cover our sins.

The apostle John records a scene in heaven featuring the Lamb of God encircled by the four living creatures and the 24 elders. The elders and the living creatures join in a triumphant new song:

> "You are worthy to take the scroll
>> and to open its seals,
> because you were slain,
>> and with your blood you purchased men for God
>> from every tribe and language and people and
>> nation.
> You have made them to be a kingdom and priests
>> to serve our God,
>> and they will reign on the earth."
>> —Revelation 5:9, 10

Hearing the song, the angel choir gathers round and

loudly sings another verse:

> "Worthy is the Lamb, who was slain,
>> to receive power and wealth and wisdom and strength
> and honor and glory and praise!" (verse 12).

The revelator tells us that as heaven echoes with praise to the Lamb, another choir composed of every creature in the universe adds its voices:

> "To him who sits on the throne and to the Lamb
>> be praise and honor and glory and power, for
>>> ever and ever!" (verse 13).

At that the four living creatures shout, "Amen," and the elders fall down and worship (verse 14).

One day we too, as the saved of earth, will join in the triumphant song of Moses and the Lamb.

Although it has been a long time since I was a goat girl, yet I can't resist at least one Bible story about goats. You have already seen that God did not always scorn goats as wicked. Goats were acceptable as sacrifices in the wilderness and Temple services of the Jews.

In fact, in one very special service, the Day of Atonement, the priests were to choose two goats. One, called the Lord's goat, they offered as a sacrifice. The blood of the Lord's goat, representing Jesus' death for us, they took into the Most Holy Place in the most solemn service of the year. It provided symbolic atonement for the whole nation.

The second goat, called Azazel, represented Satan, who was not only responsible for the entrance of sin into the universe, but who continually tempts humanity to further sin. The priests did not kill this goat. After they had offered the blood of the Lord's goat for atonement, they exiled Azazel in the wilderness, symbolizing the final and complete removal of sin from the universe (see Lev. 16).

One more Old Testament sheep story involves David, the man who wrote the shepherd's psalm, the man who walked and talked with God as he cared for his father's sheep, the man whom God Himself called a person after His own heart.

The responsibilities of being a king and the honor and praise heaped upon him tempted David into self-indulgence, and he became careless in keeping alive his daily relationship with his divine Shepherd. As the sense of God's presence faded, his conscience dulled, and he had a faithful retainer killed so that he, David, could cover up his own sin of adultery with the man's wife. God sent the prophet Nathan to David with a sheep story, one bound to touch his heart:

"There were two men in a certain town, one rich and the other poor. The rich man had a very large number of sheep and cattle, but the poor man had nothing except one little ewe lamb he had bought. He raised it, and it grew up with him and his children. It shared his food, drank from his cup and even slept in his arms. It was like a daughter to him.

"Now a traveler came to the rich man, but the rich man refrained from taking one of his own sheep or cattle to prepare a meal for the traveler who had come to him. Instead, he took the ewe lamb that belonged to the poor man and prepared it for the one who had come to him" (2 Sam. 12:1-4).

Angry at the heartlessness of the rich man, David exclaimed to Nathan, "As surely as the Lord lives, the man who did this deserves to die! He must pay for that lamb four times over, because he did such a thing and had no pity" (verses 5, 6).

"You are the man!" Nathan told the king (verse 7).

As the surprised king hung his head in shame God further chided David. "I anointed you king over Israel, and I delivered you from the hand of Saul. I gave your master's house to you, and your master's wives into your arms. I gave you the house of Israel and Judah. And if all this had been too little, *I would have given you even more.* Why did you despise the word of the Lord by doing what is evil in his eyes? You struck down Uriah the Hittite with the sword and took his wife to be your own. You killed him with the sword of the Ammonites. Now, therefore, the sword will never depart from your house, because you despised me and took the wife of Uriah the Hittite to be your own" (verses 7-10).

What a thrust to David's heart! His response was immediate: "I have sinned against the Lord" (verse 13). The humbled monarch confessed his sin, and God forgave him—but the consequences of that terrible sin have persisted throughout the entire history of the Jewish nation—and perhaps through all earth time.

Although as a grown-up I understood the reasons for choosing sheep to illustrate Christians and goats to represent the wicked, still I was reluctant to be called a sheep. If the truth were told, I suspect that many of us resist being a sheep. Our inherited tendencies are to want to go our own way rather than be part of a flock. So the lessons we can learn not only from the illustration of Jesus as the Good Shepherd but also from His experience as a sheep, dependent upon His Father as His shepherd, are invaluable to prepare us for His eternal kingdom.

> "He was oppressed and afflicted,
> yet he did not open his mouth;
> he was led like a lamb to the slaughter,
> and as a sheep before her shearers is silent,
> so he did not open his mouth."
> —Isaiah 53:7

Jesus was the lamb taken to the slaughter, and He made

no complaint. Here is my answer to my tendency to worry and grumble. If I accept my assignment to be a sheep, I will trust in my Shepherd without complaint.

Good news—I am no longer a reluctant sheep.

### *The Song of the Contented Sheep*
by David, the shepherd youth

"The Lord is my shepherd, I shall not be in want.
  He makes me lie down in green pastures,
he leads me beside quiet waters,
  he restores my soul.
He guides me in paths of righteousness
  for his name's sake.
Even though I walk
  through the valley of the shadow of death,
I will fear no evil,
  for you are with me;
your rod and your staff,
  they comfort me.
You prepare a table before me
  in the presence of my enemies.
You anoint my head with oil;
  my cup overflows.
Surely goodness and love will follow me
  all the days of my life,
and I will dwell in the house of the Lord
  forever."

—Psalm 23

## The Face of God

in

## "I Am the Shepherd and You Are My Sheep"

God's face as the Good Shepherd is a familiar one. Artists have often portrayed this beautiful metaphor on canvas. Such pictures adorn the walls of churches, homes, and hospitals. The shepherd's psalm is perhaps the best-known scripture throughout the Christian world. But what are the unique traits of a shepherd that give us a deeper look into God's character?

One of the distinctive features of Jesus' parable of the good shepherd is that He plays so many roles: He is the Good Shepherd, He is the Door, and ultimately, of course, He is the Lamb (or Sheep) who died for the sins of the world.

As the Shepherd, God chooses His sheep, leads them to pasture and water, provides them with love and companionship, protects them from marauders, and even gives His life for them. In the story of the lost sheep we see the Shepherd leaving the 99 sheep in the sheepfold and going out into the night to rescue the one lost sheep. Nothing can take us out of the Shepherd's care.

As the Door to the sheepfold, Jesus is the only way that we can become a part of God's family. Others may enter the fold by climbing over the wall or crawling under the fence, but God's true flock come in through the Door.

As the Lamb (sheep), Jesus lived 33 years in ministry and service to humanity, always representing His Father, giving us an example of true Christian living, and dying in our place the final death that we all deserve, that we might live with Him eternally.

---

\* See Ex. 12; 13.

## PART VI

## *"I Am the Vine and You Are the Branches"*

I am the true vine, and my Father is the gardener.
He cuts off every branch in me that bears no fruit,
while every branch that does bear fruit
he prunes so that it will be even more fruitful.
You are already clean because of the word
I have spoken to you.
Remain in me, and I will remain in you.
No branch can bear fruit by itself;
it must remain in the vine.
Neither can you bear fruit unless you remain in me.
I am the vine; you are the branches.
If a man remains in me and I in him,
he will bear much fruit;
apart from me you can do nothing. . . .
If you remain in me and my words remain in you,
ask whatever you wish, and it will be given you.
This is to my Father's glory, that you bear much fruit,
showing yourselves to be my disciples."

—John 15:1-8

CHAPTER 11

## *The Connection*

I am the true vine," Jesus said, "and my Father is the gardener" (John 15:1).[1] With these words Jesus began the last parable that He told His disciples before He went to the cross.

He and His disciples had eaten the Passover meal together in an upstairs room in Jerusalem. Judas, the betrayer, had left in offended haste shortly after Jesus washed the dusty feet of each of His disciples. Jesus had spent the next hour trying to prepare His dearest friends—the humbled eleven—for the horrendous events soon to take place. But they seemed not to comprehend that anything but honor awaited them, in spite of what He had told them in the past and what He related to them that night.

Now it was time to leave the room, and He led the little company away from Jerusalem up the hillside toward a place familiar to them all—the Garden of Gethsemane—where they often went to pray. The moonlight enabled them to see the way clearly, and Jesus noted a grapevine by the wayside. Perhaps the disciples would remember an object lesson. He pointed out the vine to the disciples by saying, "I am the true vine, and my Father is the gardener."

Jesus did not claim to be like the mighty oak or cedar that stood proudly alone. No, He was the vine, supported by His heavenly Father. "You, my friends, are the branches,"

Jesus added, "and if you stay connected to the vine, you will bear much fruit."

As Jesus told His last parable to the puzzled disciples they stood around Him in the moonlight with heavy hearts. It was all so confusing—just when they had hoped that Jesus was about to set up a new kingdom, it was obvious that He had no such intention at all!

"My Father is the gardener," Jesus repeated. "He cuts off every branch that does not bear fruit, and those that bear fruit He prunes so that they bear more fruit."

His parable of the vine would later have great meaning for the disciples—and down through the centuries it continues to reveal to us eternal truths about the relationship between God and humanity.

In each of the scriptural metaphors we have portrayed in this book so far, we have seen two separate parts: God and His people, the Father and His children, a Husband and His wife, a Potter and the clay, the Shepherd and the sheep. But as we look at the vine we discover that the branches are part of the vine. Separated from the vine the branches become only firewood.

In each of the five previous metaphors we have found important aspects of the intimacy that God wants to have with us. Many of the truths about God get repeated from one illustration to another with just a slight new twist. But in the story of the vine we find something new: God desires us to be a part of Him. Connected.

Jesus said it often and in varying words those last few weeks and days of His life, but the meaning was the same: "The Father and I are one; I am in Him and He is in Me. Our desire is that you allow Us to be in you and you be in Us." Definitely one vine.

The most important part of being a branch is to stay

connected. The next is to bear fruit. Both are possible only as the sap from the parent vine flows freely into every part of the branch.

As Jews, the disciples had grown up hearing the metaphor of their nation as a vineyard, cared for by the leadership that God had given them through priests, prophets, and kings. Although the Jewish leaders approached this with pride, Isaiah records how God felt about His vineyard:

> "I will sing for the one I love
>> a song about his vineyard:
> My loved one had a vineyard
>> on a fertile hillside.
> He dug it up and cleared it of stones
>> and planted it with the choicest vines.
> He built a watchtower in it
>> and cut out a winepress as well.
> Then he looked for a crop of good grapes,
>> but it yielded only bad fruit.
> 'Now you dwellers in Jerusalem and men of Judah,
>> judge between me and my vineyard.
> What more could have been done for my vineyard
>> than I have done for it?
> When I looked for good grapes,
>> why did it yield only bad?' "
>
> —Isaiah 5:1-4

Just a few days earlier Jesus had told a similar story of a man who planted a vineyard, built a wall around it, dug a winepress, and put up a watchtower. Then he rented it out to some tenant farmers to care for and went on a trip, expecting to come home to an abundant harvest of grapes. When he had a servant attempt to collect what was due the landlord, the renters flogged him. The owner dispatched another servant, and they killed him. The third they stoned. He sent more servants, only to have them treated in the same way.

Finally the man had his son go, thinking, *Surely these men will respect my son.* But the wicked tenants threw the son out of the vineyard and killed him, hoping to keep the vineyard for themselves.

Jesus ended the story with the question: "When the owner of the vineyard comes, what will he do to those tenants?" (Matt. 21:40).

The religious leaders fell into the trap Jesus had laid for them.

"He will bring those wretches to a wretched end," they replied, "and he will rent the vineyard to other tenants, who will give him his share of the crop at harvest time" (verse 41).

Jesus asked them, "Have you never read in the Scriptures:

> 'The stone the builders rejected
>     has become the capstone;
>   the Lord has done this,
>     and it is marvelous in our eyes'?"
>                                          —Matthew 21:42

"Therefore I tell you that the kingdom of God will be taken away from you and given to a people who will produce its fruit" (verse 43).

(Just a few days later those leaders sealed their own doom when they killed the Son.)

The mind-set of the disciples was similar to that of the religious leaders. As a nation they felt superior to the pagans around them. Did not Scripture teach that Israel was to be the head, not the tail (Deut. 28:13)? The disciples must have struggled with Jesus' strange teachings!

And now as they stood around Jesus in the moonlight He pointed out one lone grapevine and said, "I am the true vine and you are the branches." Silently they studied the branches. What was it that Jesus wanted them to do? What was His meaning?

As Jesus looked at His beloved friends in pity He assured them that their hearts were already clean—they were connected to Him. He knew they loved Him. For three and a half years they had listened to His words and believed that He was the Messiah. The Word of God, penetrating their hearts, had kept them clean. Now His counsel was that they remain in Him—keep trusting Him even though they couldn't see the future.

When an hour earlier He had been with them in the upper room, He had told them that He was going away. He had sought to comfort them with the promise that although He would no longer be present with them He was not leaving them alone. No, the third member of the Godhead, the Holy Spirit, would be nearer to them than Jesus had ever been able to be. The Holy Spirit, omnipresent, would be within each one of them. Yet they still did not understand.

All Jesus could do at the moment was to plant words and concepts in the minds of the disciples, knowing that the Holy Spirit would recall them to their remembrance when He was gone. Jesus knew their hearts. Oh yes, He knew they loved Him.

No doubt it was after the Resurrection that these things flooded back into their minds, and they began to grasp what Jesus had tried to teach them. Perhaps during the 40 days He was still with them they asked Jesus about the two parables, and He showed them how they fit together. Or maybe it was only after He returned to heaven and the Holy Spirit had been poured out in Pentecost power that they comprehended the message of the grapevine. The kingdom of God would be given to a people who would produce much fruit—a people vitally connected to the vine stock of Christ.

The promise of the Holy Spirit must have been a great encouragement to the disciples during the 10 days they spent in prayer after Jesus' ascension. And then came the mighty rush of the wind of the Spirit that energized them to go forth and preach the good news entrusted to them: Jesus is alive! His kingdom is in place—repent and be baptized. The disciples, attached to the Vine, now bore much fruit.

Today we need to concentrate on the lessons of the vine. Staying connected is the greatest task of modern humanity. Pressure to achieve, the world at our fingertips through the Internet, the world in our eyes and ears through television, the complexities of finances and business, the disintegration of the family—all these make it difficult to stay connected to the Vine. Distraction tends to fragment our intentions.

Jesus said: "Apart from me you can do nothing" (John 15:5).

The connection is all-important. And plugging in is quite simple. All we have to do is respond to the Holy Spirit as He woos us, showing us our unhappiness, our emptiness without God, and assuring us of the great peace and joy we will find in Him. Our response is to confess our sins, our inability to do anything good without Him, and to determine to follow wherever He leads. The Holy Spirit does the rest—gives us repentance that results in new birth into the kingdom of heaven and guidance to live a new life of service filled with fruit.

So how do we stay connected? Our choices make all the difference. Just as in a marriage, we must choose to spend time with the one we love—and that takes planning. When

I was born again at age 19, the example of my parents led me to begin each day with prayer and Bible reading.

Later, as a pastor's wife with four small children, I was shown by God that I could trust Him to do the impossible—give me time for Him in my hectic life. He awakened me every morning while my children were still asleep, even after a sleepless night with my babies, to spend wideawake time with Him in prayer and the Word of God. What a difference staying connected to God has made in my life! Without that special time with Him each morning I could never remain connected to the Vine.

Jesus told His disciples that His Father is the gardener who prunes the branches so that they will bear much fruit. Pruning involves at least two elements: cutting, which is most likely painful, and training, which may be distasteful and frustrating to our self-centered hearts. But the good news about pruning is that it is guaranteed to improve our connection to the Vine. The benefit will come immediately, even as the pruning is going on, if we recognize that it is the Gardener's hand holding the pruning shears and trust Him to do what is best for us. Even when in our grief or pain we do not realize that God's hand is in our suffering, we will later look back and thank Him for the pruning He has done. Either way, our connection with God becomes closer than it was before.

Our being a branch connected to the Vine the Gardener may cut away from our life:

- Relationships that separate us from Him or hinder us from ministry.
- Habits that slow us down in our spiritual growth or dull our understanding.
- Material possessions that consume our time and energy.

He will teach us that even our thoughts are important to Him. How can we grow in Him and bear fruit when the cares of life—stressful jobs, finances, health problems, worry—weigh us down?

In the Sermon on the Mount Jesus told the people: "Seek *first* his kingdom and his righteousness, and all these things [necessities of life] will be given to you as well. Therefore do not worry about tomorrow, for tomorrow will worry about itself. Each day has enough trouble of its own" (Matt. 6:33, 34).

Only days before Jesus told the story of the vine, He warned the people in the Temple: "Be careful, or your hearts will be weighed down with dissipation, drunkenness and the anxieties of life, and that day will close on you unexpectedly like a trap. For it will come upon all those who live on the face of the whole earth. Be always on the watch, and pray that you may be able to escape all that is about to happen, and that you may be able to stand before the Son of Man" (Luke 21:34-36).

Unbelievable as it may sound, pruning will actually produce joy—not the hilarious gaiety of the world, but the joy of a sense of God's presence. "Consider it pure joy, my brothers, whenever you face trials of many kinds, because you know that the testing of your faith develops perseverance. Perseverance must finish its work so that you may be mature and complete, not lacking anything" (James 1:2-4).

Perhaps you, like me, have gone through a painful period of pruning and wonder if life will ever be the same again. The answer is no, it never will be. But God will bring something into your life that will be a taste of heaven. Shed of all that hinders you, you will be able to taste and see the Lord's goodness in a new way.

Training the branch often accompanies the pruning.

Author Bruce Wilkinson tells of a conversation he had with the owner of a vineyard:

" 'New branches have a natural tendency to trail down and grow along the ground,' he [the vineyard owner] explained. 'But they don't bear fruit down there. When branches grow along the ground, the leaves get coated in dust. When it rains, they get muddy and mildewed. The branch becomes sick and useless.'

" 'What do you do?' I asked. 'Cut it off and throw it away?'

" 'Oh, no!' he exclaimed. 'The branch is much too valuable for that. We go through the vineyard with a bucket of water looking for those branches. We lift them up and wash them off.' He demonstrated for me with dark, callused hands. 'Then we wrap them around the trellis or tie them up. Pretty soon they're thriving.' " [2]

I'm so glad that God has shown His face in the parable of the vine. How wonderful to know that He comes after me when I'm trailing in the dirt, lifts me up, washes the dust of contact with the world from me, and fastens me to Himself, training me to remain habitually close to Him. The water He uses? The water of the Word of God. Whenever I find myself feeling estranged from God in any way, I can take up my Bible and reread the precious promises of God: how much He loves me, how He gave His life for me, how He promises that He will never never leave me alone. The soil of the world gets washed away and my relationship with God renewed.

Ellen White, in her classic *Steps to Christ,* tells us that the devil uses four ways to divert our attention from God so that we do not spend the time in communication with Him and thus keep our souls clean: (1) the pleasures of the world; (2) the cares, perplexities, and sorrows of life; (3) the faults of others; (4) our own faults and imperfections. She says:

"Commit the keeping of your soul to God, and trust in Him. Talk and think of Jesus. Let self be lost in Him. Put away all doubt; dismiss your fears. Say with the apostle Paul, 'I live; yet not I, but Christ liveth in me: and the life which I now live in the flesh I live by the faith of the Son of God, who loved me, and gave Himself for me.' Galatians 2:20. Rest in God. He is able to keep that which you have committed to Him. If you will leave yourself in His hands, He will bring you off more than conqueror through Him that has loved you."[3]

Keep your soul clean through daily Bible study and prayer. Your relationship with God depends upon what choices you make about what will occupy your mind.

In the story of the vine and the branches we find all three persons of the Godhead intimately involved. Christ is the vine, His Father is the gardener, and the Holy Spirit is the life-giving force flowing from the vine to the branches. Through the Holy Spirit our connection with the Vine is always secure.

With a sense of urgency Jesus counseled His disciples about how to stay connected to Him when He was no longer with them:

"If you love me, you will obey what I command. And I will ask the Father, and he will give you another Counselor to be with you forever—the Spirit of truth. The world cannot accept him, because it neither sees him nor knows him. But you know him, for he lives with you and will be in you. I will not leave you as orphans; I will come to you. Before long, the world will not see me anymore, but you will see me. Because I live, you also will live. On that day you will realize that I am in my Father, and you are in me, and I am in you. Whoever has my commands and obeys them, he is the one who loves me. He who loves me will be loved by my Father, and I too will love him and show myself to him" (John 14:15-21).

"I have much more to say to you, more than you can now bear. But when he, the Spirit of truth, comes, he will guide you into all truth. He will not speak on his own; he will speak only what he hears, and he will tell you what is yet to come. He will bring glory to me by taking from what is mine and making it known to you. All that belongs to the Father is mine. That is why I said the Spirit will take from what is mine and make it known to you" (John 16:12-15).

Our first assignment as a newly born Christian, connected to the vinestock of Jesus Christ, is to stay connected to the Vine. Likewise, our prime consideration as a mature Christian is to remain joined to the Vine. If we are joined to the Vine, we will bear fruit to the glory of God and His kingdom.

---

[1] Story of the vine and branches paraphrased from John 15.

[2] Bruce Wilkinson, *Secrets of the Vine* (Portland, Oreg.: Multnomah Pubs., 2001), pp. 34, 35.

[3] E. G. White, *Steps to Christ,* p. 72.

## CHAPTER 12

## *Bearing Much Fruit*

The reason we plant grapevines is to produce grapes. Jesus used this as an illustration of what He expects from born-again believers. We are to produce the fruit of righteousness in our lives.

Jesus put great importance upon the bearing of fruit. He said that any branch that does not bear fruit, the Father, as the gardener, will cut off and throw into the fire to be burned. And every branch that bears fruit, He will prune so that it will grow even more fruit.

What is the fruit that the Christian should produce? For years I thought that it consisted solely of the number of individuals each person led into God's kingdom. That made me sad—for though I had given many Bible studies to people wanting to know more about our church, I could not point to anyone whom I had actually brought to Christ. I read stories of great evangelists who guided many people to Jesus, of people who started churches in towns where there were no congregations, of people who led their whole families to the Lord. Why was it that I, an active pastor's wife, was not producing the fruit that God desired?

Then I took a new look at what Scripture teaches about fruit.

John the Baptist, whom God sent to prepare the way

for Jesus' ministry, talked about fruit bearing. When the people thronged out into the desert to listen to his preaching, he warned them that they should "produce fruit in keeping with repentance" (Matt. 3:8). "The ax is already at the root of the trees," he added, "and every tree that does not produce good fruit will be cut down and thrown into the fire" (verse 10).

True, John the Baptist was not talking about grapevines, but about fruit-bearing trees, yet it was the same principle. If you produce only foliage and no fruit, you are useless in the garden of God.

The parable of the vine and the branches is not the first place Jesus discussed fruit bearing. In the Sermon on the Mount, His first recorded sermon, He said:

"Watch out for false prophets. They come to you in sheep's clothing, but inwardly they are ferocious wolves. *By their fruit you will recognize them.* Do people pick grapes from thornbushes, or figs from thistles? Likewise every good tree bears good fruit, but a bad tree bears bad fruit. *A good tree cannot bear bad fruit, and a bad tree cannot bear good fruit.* Every tree that does not bear good fruit is cut down and thrown into the fire. Thus, by their fruit you will recognize them" (Matt. 7:15-20).

For me two principles stood out in this passage. First, fruit identifies a person as being a Christian. Without fruit you are not a Christian. Second, if you belong to Christ, you will bear good fruit. To produce bad fruit reveals that you are not a child of God.

Jesus told a parable about a man who planted a fig tree, expecting to have fruit to eat:

"A man had a fig tree, planted in his vineyard, and he went to look for fruit on it, but did not find any. So he said to the man who took care of the vineyard, 'For three years now

I've been coming to look for fruit on this fig tree and haven't found any. Cut it down! Why should it use up the soil?'

" 'Sir,' the man replied, 'leave it alone for one more year, and I'll dig around it and fertilize it. If it bears fruit next year, fine! If not, then cut it down' " (Luke 13:6-9).

In this parable the Father is the owner of the vineyard, while Jesus is the gardener. The owner had carefully visited his vineyard regularly, noticing which trees bore fruit and which did not. No doubt he kept records, for he had been especially watching one fig tree that had not produced a harvest in three years' time. He discussed the situation with the gardener, suggesting that he chop the tree down. Notice the gardener's tender concern and patience with the fruitless fig tree. He was willing to give special attention to it—provide extra cultivation and fertilizer—for one more year. But his forbearance had a time limit. The gardener said that if within the specified time the tree bore no figs, it should be removed. A tree that produces no harvest takes up space and nutrients in the soil needed by those that do bear fruit.

It became obvious to me from such Bible passages that fruit bearing is not an option for the Christian. Every Christian will bear fruit. I also began to see that the fruit the Christian produces has to include much more than winning others to Christ. Although God uses individuals as witnesses and teachers to lead people to Him, few turn to God through the intervention of one person alone. Usually conversion is a slow process, and many people act their part along the way. Although the human instrument is important, still it is ultimately the patient, loving persistence of the Holy Spirit that leads someone to Christ.

The apostle Paul gets right down to basics as he describes what true fruit is:

"But the fruit of the Spirit is love, joy, peace, patience, kindness, goodness, faithfulness, gentleness and self-control. Against such things there is no law. Those who belong to Christ Jesus have crucified the sinful nature with its passions and desires. Since we live by the Spirit, let us keep in step with the Spirit. Let us not become conceited, provoking and envying each other" (Gal. 5:22-26).

The presence of the Holy Spirit in an individual will produce a difference in the life as visible as fruit is on a vine or tree branch. It will turn a selfish person into a caring, loving Christian. Some of the best biblical examples are the eleven disciples. We see them through the gospel stories as proud, ambitious, timid, rash, or angry—depending upon their particular weaknesses. Yet dramatic changes occurred in them after Pentecost, when the power of the Holy Spirit filled their lives.

Many of us have heard the saying "An apple tree does not bear apples by trying, but because it is an apple tree." It's the same with branches—Christians bear fruit because they are branches connected to the Vine—not because they try hard to grow fruit. We can't fake it. It's true that I must *will* to live like Jesus, but it is not my will that produces fruit. Without the Spirit within me I am incapable of bearing fruit. I know by experience that my human nature is more like the other list Paul gives in the same chapter that itemizes the acts of the sinful nature. But when I set my heart toward doing what God wants me to do, I find that the Spirit works through me to walk in the footsteps of Jesus.

The fruit of the Spirit *will be visible in the life of the Spirit-filled person.* It does not mean that Spirit-filled Christians are sinless. But they are in the *process* of becoming like Jesus, and the likeness is apparent. The entire Godhead ministers to accomplish this work in each of us.

When I accept Jesus into my life through the Holy Spirit, I receive Christ's character of love.

Charles Stanley says in his book *The Wonderful Spirit-filled Life* that the evidence of fruit fills three important functions in the church:

1. The fruit attracts non-Christians to the church—fruit-bearing Christians have an inviting fragrance that draws people.

2. The fruit is like oil that keeps the church running smoothly without friction. A church may be filled with spiritually gifted people, yet unless they are also fruit-bearing Christians, they will not be able to work together in harmony and will accomplish little for God's kingdom.

3. Being a fruit-bearing Christian protects us from evil around us. Whereas our attempts to produce the fruit of the Spirit on our own are futile, God can accomplish the impossible. While our love is breakable and subject to change, God's love is unchangeable. No longer will our human emotions control our thoughts and behavior, for God has given us the mind of Christ. God's plan is to develop in us a character that can endure anything.

Stanley goes on to describe the fruit exhibited by the Spirit-filled Christian:

Love—for those who do not love in return.

Joy—even in the midst of painful circumstances.

Peace—when something you were counting on doesn't come through.

Patience—when things aren't going fast enough for you.

Kindness—toward those who treat you unkindly.

Goodness—toward those who have been intentionally insensitive to you.

Faithfulness—when friends have proved unfaithful.

Gentleness—toward those who have handled you roughly.

Self-control—in the midst of intense temptation.*

Impossible? Idealistic? Yes, on our own it is. But we need not be alone. Filled with the Spirit, we are to reveal to the world fruit that is the face of God.

The apostle Paul emphasized the blessings given to fruit-bearing Christians:

"And this is my prayer: that your love may abound more and more in knowledge and depth of insight, so that you may be able to discern what is best and may be pure and blameless until the day of Christ, *filled with the fruit of righteousness* that comes through Jesus Christ—to the glory and praise of God" (Phil. 1:9-11).

"For this reason, since the day we heard about you, we have not stopped praying for you and asking God to fill you with the knowledge of his will through all spiritual wisdom and understanding. And we pray this in order that you may live a life worthy of the Lord and may please him in every way: *bearing fruit in every good work,* growing in the knowledge of God, being strengthened with all power according to his glorious might so that you may have great endurance and patience, and joyfully giving thanks to the Father, who has qualified you to share in the inheritance of the saints in the kingdom of light. For he has rescued us from the dominion of darkness and brought us into the kingdom of the Son he loves, in whom we have redemption, the forgiveness of sins" (Col. 1:9-14).

The author of the book of James adds: "But the wisdom that comes from heaven is first of all pure; then peace-loving, considerate, submissive, *full of mercy and good fruit, impartial and sincere.* Peacemakers who sow in peace raise a harvest of righteousness" (James 3:17, 18).

What a glorious picture of God the church would portray if we were all Spirit-filled Christians! That is exactly how the Lord plans to reveal Himself to the world—through Spirit-filled, fruit-bearing Christians.

What does this involve in terms of intimacy with God?

It means that God is not content with living outside of us, speaking to us from a mountain or through our pastor. No, God will be satisfied only when He is inside us and we are inside Him—the deepest intimacy possible. The vine and the branch story portrays not two people in close communion, but one in thought, action, and purpose.

It all sounds great, doesn't it? Thriving, fruit-bearing branches, a vibrant living vineyard. The reality is, though, that there are many dying branches on the Lord's vine. What happens to those? Jesus plainly stated that the non-fruit-bearing branches wither away and will get cut off and thrown into the fire (John 15:6). Is this the end for that branch, or is there any hope for a cutoff bough?

I've discovered that the Bible speaks in several places of those hacked off and thrown into the fire. In the margin of my Bible, right beside Jesus' comment about the withered branches, I've written: *"There is even hope for branches thrown in the fire."* And then I've added two Bible references: Jude 23 and Zechariah 3:2.

Jude 23 tells us to "snatch others from the fire and save them." The prophet Zechariah had a vision of Joshua the high priest standing before God, with Satan beside him to accuse him. How does God respond to the situation? "The Lord said to Satan, 'The Lord rebuke you, Satan! The Lord, who has chosen Jerusalem, rebuke you! Is not this man a burning stick snatched from the fire?'" (Zech. 3:2).

Although it may not work on a grapevine—and thus is not a part of the parable—it seems to me that the kingdom

144

of God has hope even for a branch the Gardener has cut off and thrown into the fire. What hope? That someone will snatch it out of the fire. How is that possible? Most assuredly by intercessory prayer—but also by the open extension of unconditional love.

The apostle Paul was just such a branch, prayed for—or against—by the entire newborn Christian church as he persecuted the believers in Jerusalem. Ananias extended him love and acceptance in Damascus, and later Barnabas, and finally the disciples, accepted him. That burning stick snatched from the fire became the apostle Paul, one of the greatest Christian evangelists of all time, bearing much fruit to the glory of God.

"Through Jesus, therefore, let us continually offer to God a sacrifice of praise—the fruit of lips that confess his name. And do not forget to do good and to share with others, for with such sacrifices God is pleased" (Heb. 13:15, 16).

The Face of God

in

"I Am the Vine and You Are the Branches"

Perhaps the face of God is clearer in this story than in any other. Without the sturdy root and stalk of the vine the branches would wither and die. The two parts of the relationship described in the parable are actually one. One plus one equals one.

As in each of the other metaphors we have studied in this book, we can divide the story of the vine and branches into two aspects: God's and humanity's. God's part is to provide life and growth, to prune and train. The human part is to stay connected to the Vine and to bear fruit.

Yet the Vine and branches constitute one plant. We can easily delineate the entire Godhead in this parable: Jesus, the Vine from which the branches grow; the Father, the Gardener who does the pruning and training; the Spirit, the indwelling life flowing through the branches to keep them fresh and fruit-bearing.

Our responsibility as branches is to remain united to the Vine at all times.

How do we stay connected? By spending daily time with God in personal Bible study and prayer.

What is the result of staying connected? We will bear much fruit.

What keeps us from being contaminated by the evil around us? The Word of God cleans our hearts from fleshly and worldly thoughts and fills us with God's thoughts. This will, in turn, lead us to produce fruit to God's glory—a holy Spirit-filled life of ministry: worship, intercessory prayer, teaching, and loving service.

---

* Charles Stanley, *The Wonderful Spirit-filled Life* (Nashville: Thomas Nelson, Inc., 1995), p. 108.

CONCLUSION:

## *He Wants Us to Ask Him for More*

We've seen God as a leader of people, as a loving Father with His obedient Son, as a strong and steadfast Husband eager to come for His bride, as a Potter molding the clay, as a Shepherd leading and caring for His sheep, and as a Vine connected to His branches. What is the most important concept about the relationship between God and humanity that you have learned from these six metaphors?

Very likely the answer to that question will be different for each of us.

But for me it is the discovery that I need never be alone: Scripture shows us that God's interest and involvement with humanity is all about developing a permanent relationship. When God chose me as His person, His bride, His child, He promised that He would never leave me. Alone, I am speechless, terrified, and lost. Joined to God, I have all the resources of heaven available. From Scripture I've caught a glimpse of those resources, and they are more abundant than I could have imagined!

Through the relationship with God described in Bible metaphors, I have found someone to talk to! Someone who listens, who answers me. Prayer is not just words flung out into the universe with the hope that someone will hear them. Prayer is conversation with a God who is the embodiment of all six metaphors we have been studying. And He has wonderful plans for you and me:

- To make us the persons we long to be.
- To enlarge our understanding and abilities.
- To use us in ministry with Him in ways we have never dreamed of.
- To deepen the companionship we have with Him here on earth.

God did all this for the apostle Paul, and Paul spent the rest of his life encouraging others to also reach out and grasp the abundant resources that heaven has to change us and make us faithful stewards in the kingdom of God. A passage from 1 Corinthians 2 opened my eyes to my personal part in God's plan for my oneness with Him:

"When I came to you, brothers, I did not come with eloquence or superior wisdom as I proclaimed to you the testimony about God. For I resolved to know nothing while I was with you except Jesus Christ and him crucified. I came to you in weakness and fear, and with much trembling. My message and my preaching were not with wise and persuasive words, but with a demonstration of the Spirit's power, so that your faith might not rest on men's wisdom, but on God's power" (1 Cor. 2:1-5).

Did you catch what God is asking of us? Nothing. That's right, nothing *except* Jesus Christ and Him crucified. My weakness and fear—and even trembling—are part of God's plan. When I speak or when I write, lacking wise or persuasive words, that too comprises part of God's plan. For the only thing that matters is that there be a demonstration of the Spirit's power in the place where I speak or for the readers of my books. And there will be if I have that intimate relationship with God promised to us through the medium of prayer.

Paul goes on to say that although he doesn't trust his own wisdom or eloquent words, it doesn't mean that he doesn't have a message of wisdom to present—but it is not the wisdom of this world. The apostle's message is God's secret wisdom, hidden away for us to find in the Word of God. He says that the seemingly important people of the world haven't understood this wisdom—or they wouldn't have crucified the Son of God (verses 6-8). Then he quotes a passage from Isaiah:

> "No eye has seen,
>> no ear has heard,
> no mind has conceived
>> what God has prepared for those who love him."
>>> —1 Corinthians 2:9

I've heard this scripture quoted often as a promise of the wonders that God has in mind for His redeemed in heaven and in the new earth. I'm sure that it is true when used in that way—surely God has marvelous things planned for eternity. But when Isaiah originally wrote the words Paul later quoted, he used the mighty acts God did in the past for His people, Israel, as an example of what the Lord will do for all who trust in Him. The prophet did not mean that we can't expect God to act until everything is made new—Isaiah believed God's mighty power was available right then:

> "For when you did awesome things that we did
>> not expect,
>> you came down, and the mountains trembled
>> before you.
> Since ancient times no one has heard,
>> no ear has perceived,
> no eye has seen any God besides you,
>> who acts on behalf of those who wait for him.

You come to the help of those who gladly do right,
who remember your ways."

—Isaiah 64:3-5

When Paul quotes Isaiah's words, he adds, "But God has revealed it to us by his Spirit" (1 Cor. 2:10).

What had God revealed to Paul and his fellow Christians? Mighty acts of power that eyes have not seen and ears have not heard.

The apostle goes on to clarify what he meant when he quoted Isaiah:

"The Spirit searches all things, even the deep things of God. For who among men knows the thoughts of a man except the man's spirit within him? In the same way no one knows the thoughts of God except the Spirit of God. We have not received the spirit of the world but the Spirit who is from God, that we may understand what God has freely given us. This is what we speak, not in words taught us by human wisdom but in words taught by the Spirit, expressing spiritual truths in spiritual words" (verses 10-13).

Could it be that Paul is saying that God has hidden treasures in His Word that the Holy Spirit longs to reveal to us? Treasures of truth about God and His desire for us? Treasures about the depth of the relationship He wants to have with us? New duties and new truths for the Christian?

The Holy Spirit, who comprehends divine thoughts better than we understand our own minds, wants to explain God's words to us!

Now is the time to set our faces toward God in faith and determination to obey Him at all costs. He can change us from weak, indecisive, and fearful to strong, firm, and faithful—the kind of people who would give our lives for truth. God wants to fill us with zeal and courage. The key to finding such treasures is to spend time with Him in Bible study and prayer.

"The Lord is exalted, for he dwells on high;
    he will fill Zion with justice and righteousness.
He will be the sure foundation for your times,
    a rich store of salvation and wisdom and
        knowledge;
    the fear of the Lord is the key to this treasure."
                      —Isaiah 33:5, 6

God has *much more* planned for us than routine prayer and Bible study. He wants us to find the "rich store of salvation and wisdom and knowledge" that is available to us. The Lord wants us to get excited about the reality of a relationship with Him. I am not speaking primarily of emotion—though our response will surely contain emotion—but I am thinking of the added consciousness of God's presence, the enlarging of our understanding, the desire to spend more time in prayer, the freedom we find in prayer, and the increased ability to share what we are learning with others.

Forgive me if I sound as though I know all this by experience. Actually I am just like you—longing for more than I have ever known before. No doubt you—as I—have had times when God has blessed you with terrific insights that have changed your lives, and you have shared them with those around you. But God wants this experience to be the norm for His people, not the exception. I know that God has *much more* for us today than we are experiencing. We can greet each new day with expectancy—can come to every Bible study and prayer session in anticipation of receiving a blessing.

There is a story I tell almost everywhere I speak, one that I've included in one of my other books, but it fits so well with this chapter that I'll recount it again.

One morning in my prayer time I reviewed in my mind the many insights God had given me during the past few months. It had definitely been a time of growth for me as a Christian. Almost overwhelmed with what God had revealed to me, I began to pray.

"Lord, You have blessed me so greatly with all these insights that You don't need to show me anything more for a long time. Anytime I need a blessing, I'll just remember one of the wonderful things You've taught me these past few months."

Because I felt that I was complimenting God for all He had done for me, I was surprised to sense His displeasure.

Distinctly I heard the inward voice of the Holy Spirit.

"You give yourself more credit than you do Me for liking to give."

Bewildered, I asked, "What do You mean, Lord? I don't understand."

His reply amazed me—just four words: "Remember peach ice cream."

Puzzled, I wondered if I had misunderstood. Surely God wouldn't talk to me about peach ice cream!

You see, homemade peach ice cream is a summer favorite of our whole family. Several times throughout the peach season we plan a special occasion centering around making ice cream.

Our recipe is simple: 10 or 12 (depending on the size) juicy ripe peaches and two quarts of half-and-half (or nondairy substitute). Put peaches in boiling water for about a minute until the skin loosens—peel them, remove pits, cut peaches into fourths, place one third of the peaches in the blender with one third of the half-and-half, sugar to taste, and add a touch of lemon juice to bring out the flavor. Blend until smooth. Pour into freezer can. Repeat two more times with the remainder of the peaches and liquid. This recipe fills our six-quart freezer perfectly.

Our freezer is the old-fashioned hand-cranked kind. My husband and sons are all experts at perfectly layering the rock salt and crushed ice so that the ice cream will freeze just right. (Note from my husband: two inches of crushed ice plus a generous eighth inch of rock salt for each layer.) Then they turn the handle slowly and steadily to ensure smooth, fluffy ice cream.

When we remove the lid, the whole family gathers around to watch. "Oh-h," we gasp in unison at the delectable contents.

Because we are so fond of our peach ice cream, we like to share our enjoyment with friends. But we've discovered something amazing to us—not everyone likes our ice cream! Some people are so familiar with commercial brands that they find ours too peachy and not sweet enough.

Of course, most people are much too polite to tell us that. So I've learned to serve small amounts of ice cream to those who have not eaten our version before. Then my husband and I (and whoever of the family is nearby) cautiously watch to see if we can tell if they like it. (Of course, we observe them on the sly—out of the corners of our eyes—so they won't notice. We don't want to embarrass them.) But often it is hard to tell—so when they have finished the small bowl of ice cream, we take the next step.

"Would you like some more?" one of us will tentatively ask.

Sometimes the answer is "No thanks. That was delicious, but I've had enough."

My husband and I signal each other with our eyes: "Too bad—they didn't like our ice cream."

But other times we find fellow peach lovers who exclaim, without even being asked, "What delicious ice cream! May I have some more?" Then our whole family rejoices. These people have shared with us in a special family tradition. It's a moment to treasure.

As I reminisced about our peach ice cream I heard God's inward voice again. "That's the way I am," He told me. "I love to give. Don't be content with your small bowlful of blessings. Ask Me for more."

But God had more to teach me. He showed me that it was as if I took the insights He had given me and wrapped them up in tissue paper and put them away in a drawer to remove now and then to enjoy again.

"Take those truths I've given you out of the drawer," He counseled me. "Unwrap them and hang them on the walls of your memory so they'll be where you can remember them often—and where you can easily share them with others.

"And then," He added, "I'd love it if you'd ask Me for more."

I was so excited about what God had just told me that I burst out of the room where I was having my devotions and into where my husband was studying for his Sabbath sermon. He looked up from his desk in surprise as I almost shouted, "He wants us to ask for more. God wants to give us more!"

The following quotations reinforced the concept in my mind:

"God wants our minds to expand. He desires to put His grace upon us. We may have a *feast of good things every day;* for God can open the whole treasure of heaven to us." [1]

"The gifts of Jesus are ever fresh and new. The feast that He provides for the soul never fails to give satisfaction and joy. Each new gift increases the capacity of the receiver to appreciate and enjoy the blessings of the Lord. He gives grace for grace. There can be no failure of supply. If you abide in Him, the fact that you receive a rich gift today insures the reception of a richer gift tomorrow."[2]

That is what this book is all about. Within the relationship we've been talking about, God is longing to give us more! He wishes to reveal the *face of Jesus* to us in all our daily activities.

"For God, who said, 'Let light shine out of darkness,' made his light shine in our hearts to give us the light of the knowledge of the glory of God in the face of Christ" (2 Cor. 4:6).

---

[1] Ellen G. White, *Selected Messages* (Washington, D.C.: Review and Herald Pub. Assn., 1958), book 1, p. 416.

[2] White, *The Desire of Ages,* p. 148.

## *We Shall See Him Face to Face*

Two kingly figures stand companionably in the shade of a giant oak, watching the activity surrounding a glorious city. Laughing groups of people walk in and out of the open gates. The eyes of the two in the shadow of the tree are intent upon the people spread out across the countryside from the city to the hills beyond. Some groups easily climb the gentle hills to see what is beyond, and others, more ambitious, set out to scale the very highest peaks.

"Can You believe it, Son?" God the Father exclaims. "It's all over. *Sin is no more.*"

"No more tears," responds the Son, wiping one from His face.

"Except for happy tears," the Father agrees, swiping away a tear or two of His own.

"No more death," the Son continues, then adds, "or fear. I sometimes think that fear was almost the greatest enemy. Fear kept people from responding to Us."

The Father looks serious. "Do You think it was worth it all?" He asks the Son. "All the pain, all those years?"

"Surely You're not serious, Father," the Son exclaims, looking intently into His Father's face. "No, of course You're not," the Son decides as He sees His Father's smile. "You're only joking. We both agree that having a happy, holy universe is worth all the pain."

The Son holds out His hands palms up and, looking from hand to hand, adds, "If it weren't for these scars in My hands, I think I would forget those long years of agony—the joy of what We have now is so very great!"

Silence reigns between the Holy Two as both remember the price paid for Their happiness.

"But I don't want to forget," the Son remarks. "I want to remember the keen joy of watching a human respond to the offer of salvation. I want to remember the joyful songs the angels sang at times like that. I want to remember the prayers and the love our human family sent heavenward, even in their darkest hours. And I want to remember how they learned to listen in their inmost hearts as the Holy Spirit spoke for all three of Us. What precious conversation We enjoyed heart-to-heart with Our creation, even while sin existed!"

"Yes," the Father comments, "I remember the clouds of prayers that ascended up before Our throne from earth's prayer warriors. Oh, what a joy it is to be able to talk face to face with these loved ones now!"

"No more hiding in a dark cloud," laughs the Son. "And the angels love being able to interact freely with the special people they guarded throughout their time on earth."

"Freedom, that's what it is," the Father speaks slowly but with authority. "The whole universe is finally totally free."

"I love this new earth." The Son throws His arms wide to encompass the vista. "I think it's even lovelier than when We created it the first time."

"You know why that is so, don't You?" the Father muses. "Not even a trace of evil remains in the entire universe. The colors are brighter; the air sparkles in the sunlight; sound vibrates with holiness. No evil lurks even in the edges of time."

The Father and Son gaze around them at the glorious sights. They see the people enjoying the beauties of nature. Together they watch the squirrels and other ground and tree creatures, the bright plumage of the birds as they fly in and out of the branches of the trees. Birdsong fills the air.

"I feel like singing Myself!" the Father exclaims.

The Son readily agrees. "Let's rejoice over this marvelous family finally safely home with Us for all eternity."

A soft, sweet humming fills the air.

Both the Father and the Son begin to laugh. "I knew the Holy Spirit was close by," the Father says. "How He too loves to sing!"

The Holy Three begin to sing a song so sweet it is impossible to put it into human words. Soon more voices join the song.

"The Martyrs' Choir," the Holy Spirit whispers. Still the music swells as another choir begins to sing.

"The 144,000!" the Son exclaims.

"Listen," the Father says, "I hear several more choirs!"

"The universe is getting involved in Our song," shouts the Holy Spirit in excitement. "I recognize those voices. They are from some of the farthest planets in the universe. Listen to the music!"

The trees begin to sway with the rhythm, and the wind whistles the melody, while thunder underscores the transitions. The birds sing arias that interweave throughout the verses. The angelic choir renders a haunting counterpart.

The Holy Three sing of their joy in face-to-face communion with the beings They so love. They celebrate the beauty of the redeemed bride of Christ. The created ones praise God for His never-failing, unending love and the price paid to rid the universe of sin.

The music swells higher and higher, fuller and fuller, as

more and more voices join in the singing. A group of jubilant hikers, singing as they return from the hills, spot the Trio in the shade of the lofty trees and hurry toward Them with eager smiles.

The Father and Son smile lovingly at each other and then turn joyously toward the people, opening wide Their arms to greet them.

"Oh, My people," God the Father whispers huskily, "I will always be your God, and you will be My people throughout all eternity!"

"How beautiful you all are," murmurs the Son, "My darling, My bride!"

Together Father and Son and Holy Spirit announce in reverent voices, "Our children are all home, never to be separated from Us again!"

John the revelator describes this incredible scene: "Then I saw a new heaven and a new earth, for the first heaven and the first earth had passed away, and there was no longer any sea. I saw the Holy City, the new Jerusalem, coming down out of heaven from God, prepared as a bride beautifully dressed for her husband. And I heard a loud voice from the throne saying, 'Now the dwelling of God is with men, and he will live with them. They will be his people, and God himself will be with them and be their God. He will wipe every tear from their eyes. There will be no more death or mourning or crying or pain, for the old order of things has passed away.'

"He who was seated on the throne said, 'I am making everything new!' Then he said, 'Write this down, for these words are trustworthy and true.'

"He said to me [John]: 'It is done. I am the Alpha and the Omega, the Beginning and the End. To him who is thirsty I will give to drink without cost from the spring of the water of life. He who overcomes will inherit all this, and I will be his God and he will be my son'" (Rev. 21:1-7).

And how will it be for us, the redeemed ones?

"Now we see but a poor reflection as in a mirror; *then we shall see face to face.* Now I know in part; *then I shall know fully, even as I am fully known*" (1 Cor. 13:12).